BLIND SPOTS

SOLVING HIDDEN BUSINESS PROBLEMS

Athena Alliance Members

iUniverse LLC
Bloomington

BLIND SPOTS
SOLVING HIDDEN BUSINESS PROBLEMS

Copyright © 2013 Athena Alliance Members.

All rights reserved. No part of this book may be used or reproduced by any means, graphic, electronic, or mechanical, including photocopying, recording, taping or by any information storage retrieval system without the written permission of the publisher except in the case of brief quotations embodied in critical articles and reviews. Requests for permission or further information should be addressed to Cindy Stradling.

This publication is designed to provide accurate and authoritative information in regard to the subject matter covered. It is sold with the understanding that neither the author nor the publisher is engaged in rending legal, accounting or other professional service. If legal advice or other expert assistant is required, the service of a competent professional person should be sought.

While the authors have used the best of their efforts in writing this book, they make no representations or warranties with respect to the accuracy or completeness of the contents of this book and specifically disclaim any implied warranties. No warranties may be created or extended by sales representatives or written sales materials. The advice and strategies contained in this may not be suitable for you. You should consult with a professional where appropriate. Neither the author nor Athena Training and Consulting Inc. shall be liable for any loss of profit or any other commercial or personal damages, including but not limited to special, incidental, consequential, or other damages.

iUniverse books may be ordered through booksellers or by contacting:

iUniverse
1663 Liberty Drive
Bloomington, IN 47403
www.iuniverse.com
1-800-Authors (1-800-288-4677)

Because of the dynamic nature of the Internet, any web addresses or links contained in this book may have changed since publication and may no longer be valid. The views expressed in this work are solely those of the author and do not necessarily reflect the views of the publisher, and the publisher hereby disclaims any responsibility for them.

Any people depicted in stock imagery provided by Thinkstock are models, and such images are being used for illustrative purposes only.

Certain stock imagery © Thinkstock.

ISBN: 978-1-4759-9653-1 (sc)
ISBN: 978-1-4759-9655-5 (e)

Library of Congress Control Number: 2013911578

Printed in the United States of America.

iUniverse rev. date: 7/1/2013

Table of Contents

Introduction vii

Prologue ix

Blind Spot One Networking Without Connecting 1

Blind Spot Two Leading Without a Personal Brand 11

Blind Spot Three Neglecting to Develop Your Direct Managers 23

Blind Spot Four Forgetting the "Customer" in Customer Service 33

Blind Spot Five Building Teams Without Communication 45

Blind Spot Six Ignoring Health and Safety at the Office 59

Blind Spot Seven Writing Without a Purpose 67

Blind Spot Eight Talking Without Listening 75

Blind Spot Nine Not Planning for Family Emergencies 83

Blind Spot Ten Presenting Without Authenticity 91

Blind Spot Eleven Selling Without Understanding Needs 101

Blind Spot Twelve Not Engaging Your Remote Workers 109

Epilogue 119

Afterword: Working with Athena 121

Afterword: Working With Writers 123

About the Authors 125

Introduction

Life is a lot like driving.

Most of us have a destination we're trying to get to: a goal we'd like to reach. But there are hazards along the way that can delay our plans, or even derail our entire trip. Where are these hazards? That's the tricky part: they're mostly hidden in the blind spots in our vision.

That's why, sometimes, it's helpful to have people driving with you who can point out those blind spots, and help you get to your destination quickly and safely.

At the Athena Alliance, blind spots are our business.

The Athena Alliance is an international group of professional trainers, coaches, and industry experts, united by our commitment to deliver the best to our clients. Our partners have decades of experience in their chosen fields, and are passionate about spreading that experience to businesses and professionals worldwide. Together, we've pioneered a "Perfect Fit" system, where we match up companies and professionals with multiple alliance partners to help them develop through challenges, and make their workplaces more engaging.

That's why we wrote this book.

Blind Spots is a professional guide written by ten members of the Athena Alliance. The book addresses the common problems we've seen professionals deal with in their careers, and offers our solutions to these challenges.

In Blind Spots, you'll meet Russell Baxter and his Protégé, Amir. You'll also meet many of the Athena Alliance members, and see them help Russell out as he develops from an uncertain, new CEO, to a master of his business. Russell Baxter is fictional, but the Athena Alliance is real. For more information on the alliance members who authored this book, you can check out the biographies at the end of the book. For more information on the Athena Alliance, you can visit athenatrainingandconsulting.com.

Prologue

Amir had a problem. This problem currently came in the form of a toaster.

The toaster sat on his desk, bathed in afternoon sunlight. Its body was bright, slightly dusty chrome. Amir could see his face in it. The face of the new CEO.

Well, at least he still had his looks.

The reason the toaster bothered him was the black square on its side. The square was soft plastic. When Amir pressed the square with his thumb, a faint green splotch rose up under the impression.

"Nancy." He muttered.

Amir jammed the toasted under his arm. He stalked out of his office with the device's power cord dragging behind him.

"Nancy?" He called.

Nancy's office was two doors down from Amir's, separated by a boardroom. Her door was open, and Amir caught a glimpse of Nancy typing something inside.

"Miss Vice President!" He called. He rapped on the door as he entered.

Nancy Saunders was Vice President at Prism. A small, fifty-year old woman with red hair and a thing for gold-rimmed glasses. As Amir entered, her head popped up from her computer screen.

Amir held the toaster out to her. "You remember everything; why does our toaster have an LCD screen on it?"

Nancy's forehead wrinkled. "I believe... it's for Twitter updates."

"Twitter updates." Amir said. "On a toaster?"

"Wait a minute. I do remember this." Nancy stood up and stretched out her hands. Amir gave her the toaster.

She twirled it around and inspected a sticker on the bottom. "This is a prototype. It was pitched… seven years ago? Anyway, it never went to market."

Nancy raised her eyebrow at him. "Have you been going through the stacks?"

Amir sighed and pinched the bridge of his nose. Prism's specialty was low-energy kitchen appliances. The stacks were the company name for the warehouse of prototypes that they'd built, but never released to the public. Yesterday Amir had drove off from work an hour early to Vaughan, where the warehouse was, to look through the prototypes.

"Let's just say…" Amir said. "That I'm looking for ideas where the company can grow."

Nancy smiled. "Here's another thing I remember. When I was head of HR and signed off to hire you, I noticed you had a stellar interview, great ideas, but you could get wound up about things when you're nervous."

Amir clapped his hands on his sides. "Maybe I've been a little wound up," he admitted. "The new job might just be a bit overwhelming."

"You're going to do fine." Nancy said. "And you don't have to prove anything. You'll be a great CEO when Russell goes."

Nancy handed back the toaster. Amir tucked it under his arm.

"Now," she winked at him. "Speaking of our dear leader, Russell came by when you were meeting with the sales team. He wants to see you when you've got a minute."

*

The door to Russell's office was half-closed. Amir knocked lightly, and peered inside.

Russell stood at the end of his office, looking down into the parking lot. He held his phone to his ear, his elbow cupped in his hand.

Russell glanced over his shoulder. Amir waved.

"Oh, he's here." Russell said. "Let me call you back."

"Sorry," Amir said. "I didn't mean to interrupt. Important call?"

Russell smiled, and shook his head. He slipped his Blackberry back into his holster. "Just an old friend. Come on. Let's get some fresh air."

Amir followed him out of the office, keeping a pace behind him.

Let's get some fresh air. That was Russ: relaxed, at peace, somehow phenomenally successful. He'd been CEO of Prism for ten years. In that time he'd rebranded the company as *the* producer of low-energy, environmentally-friendly kitchen appliances, and driven sales up from 1.2 million to over 30 million. Russell was kind to his employees, a smooth conversationalist, and a dear friend to Amir. He was everything Amir wanted to be.

"Nadine okay?" Russell asked as they waited at the elevator. Nadine was Amir's daughter.

"Oh, yeah. She's coming back in a few weeks." Amir said.

The elevator dinged open. They entered, and Russell pushed the button for the ground floor.

"And then..." Russell looked up at the ceiling. "Let's see. She's at U of T, so she'll be graduating at Convocation Hall in a month or so, right? That's a great accomplishment Amir. Give her my congrats."

Amir grinned. "You bet."

Amir had tried to pin down the aura that his boss gave off for a long time. After years of trying, he'd never figured it out, but he saw a hint of it in how Russell moved. He didn't walk like a general—all straight and stiff. Instead, he ambled about—feet splaying out without a care if there was ground beneath them or not.

Russell Baxter. CEO of Prism. A sixty-year old man with a predilection for sweater-vests and suspenders. Thinning red hair and a bit of a belly. He looked absolutely normal. Nothing to predict that he'd be as successful as he was.

Their elevator stopped. The doors slid open, revealing the lobby to the building.

The lobby looked a lot like Prism's kitchen appliances: clean, white and modern. Russell waved at the security guard on duty, and ambled to the big glass doors that lead to the courtyard.

"You know, when I first started working at here, we were holed up in a rented office at the edge of the GTA." Russell said. He held the door open to Amir.

"I saw the photos."

Russell chuckled to himself. "And the only way to get lunch was to either bring it from home or eat at Café Stavros."

Amir had also heard that it was so close to the airport that the planes could brush the building. That was probably an exaggeration.

They came out into the courtyard. The Prism office was built like an old villa: offices all around, with a square in the middle for a garden.

The courtyard path was grey gravel, winding through trees and a bocce ground where some of the older employees played during lunch. Russell ambled onto the path, heading towards a bench.

"Stavros had gold teeth." Russell continued, musingly. "I'm pretty sure he was running a money-laundering front, actually."

Russell launched into a story about how he once ate some spanakopita at Café Stavros and saw some scary-looking men in the kitchen. Amir looked up at the sky. It was a bright, windless day. He closed his eyes and breathed. He liked Russell, but he wondered if there was a point to this speech.

"Yep." Russell said. "There's a point to this speech."

Amir snapped out of his reverie and looked back at Russell.

Russell smiled. "That move—from our office to this building. From a startup to a business. From an idea to a livelihood. It didn't happen by itself."

Russell tapped the side of head. "Hard work, intelligence and... something else. And since you'll be in my shoes soon enough, I figured you might just benefit from an old man's stories."

Russell put his hand on Amir's shoulder.

"Look, Amir: ninety percent of what makes a business successful is easily attainable if you try hard enough. You've got your MBA programs, your Stephen Covey, your technical experience, and your intuition. If you use your brain, ninety percent of all the knowledge you need is pretty easy to come across."

"But there's a ten percent." Amir said. "What's that?"

"Blind spots." Russell said.

Amir looked at Russell blankly.

"It's just—stuff." Russell said. He waggled his hands for emphasis. "Stuff that you don't think about. It might drain your productivity, catch you by surprise, or just prevent you from performing at your best. Stuff you can't see. Blind spots."

They came to a stone bench in the middle of the garden. Russell shooed away a squirrel and sat down. He patted the space next to him.

"So that's how you got here?" Amir asked. He sat down. The stone felt cold beneath him. "You learned to check your blind spots?"

Russell nodded. "But I didn't do it alone."

BLIND SPOT ONE
Networking Without Connecting

"I first learned about blind spots after meeting a very interesting group of people." Russell said. "It's an interesting story, if you're willing to hear it."

Two men walked past Amir and Russell. Each walked in step with the other, with identical key cards clipped to their waist. They were talking on mobile headsets while simultaneously working on their tablets. Russell chuckled at the men—two colleagues, disconnected, even though they were walking right next to each other.

Amir nodded. "I'd love to."

Russell rubbed his palms on the rough cement of the bench, leaned back, and began his story.

"It all started at a networking event…"

★

It was a cold October night in Toronto. I was walking down Chestnut Street after parking my Saturn—I drove a Saturn back then—in a parking garage on Spadina Road.

I was headed to the Hemisphere Hotel, a small business-class hotel run by the university. The hotel stood at the end of Chestnut Street, backed by the Old City Hall.

The hotel looked across a park, and a square that hosted a farmer's market in the mornings. They were both dark and empty now, but the Hemisphere was open and bustling.

As soon as I walked inside the hotel, I knew I'd have a problem.

"Oh my," I gasped.

The hotel was full of people.

People, filing into lines that stretched across the foyer. People, swinging expensive handbags and shiny leather briefcases. People, exchanging shiny white business cards faster than dealers on the Vegas strip.

I'm not normally shy of crowds, but this was a *mob*.

I wandered around the foyer for a while, and found the line I belonged to: a queue of men and women wearing suits, trading cards, and chatting. The line led to a fold-out table where the organizers were ticking names off a long list.

I felt a tap on my shoulder.

"Excuse me. Do you need sales-boosting software?"

I turned around. A short, square woman glared up at me. She wore the strangest necklace I'd ever seen. Except, it wasn't a necklace. It was a name tag, stuffed with business cards. The name tag read: Donna Jones. It was bound around her neck with a black lanyard. The words *Fourth Quarter Sales* ran up the lanyard in white lettering.

"Um," I tore my eyes off the unconventional jewelry. "Actually my company—my name's Russell by the way—my head of human resources—her name's Nancy—she thought it would be a good idea to attend this thing so I could get some ideas for customer service. So—"

"What browser do you use?" The woman interrupted. She reached up to her name tag and flicked one of her cards from the plastic pocket. Without breaking eye contact, she handed one to me. "If you use Internet Explorer, I can guarantee you that our software will increase your optimization in any sales environment."

"... What?" I asked.

"Are you not familiar with the paradigm of high-impact technology innovation in online sales environments?" She asked. She folded her arms and looked at me like I'd just failed a test.

I mumbled something and, confused, I slowly turned away. The woman shook her head at me and started talking to the person behind her.

The registration line moved fast. I reached the front in a few seconds. A man with a clipboard beamed at me. "Hi there! Name and company?"

I leaned forward on the table. "Russell Baxter," I murmured. I pulled out a printout. "My company name is Prism. I have my registration information here."

The man at the desk nodded and handed me a name tag. "Through the hallway and into the Rose Suite. Have fun!"

I left the line with my name tag clipped to my suit pocket. I could still hear the sales-software-lady, Donna. She was directing her buzzwords to the registration desk.

I made my way to the Rose Suite. More people: men in power-suits, women in shoulder-pads. More screechy laughter and tired smiles.

I decided this would be a fine time for a drink.

I found the bar at the end of the room, populated by a silent group of professionals—my introverted comrades—who'd decided playing with their phones was better than learning about the paradigms of high-impact innovation—whatever that was. It felt like comfortable defeat to join them, but in the end, I chose to hang around these quiet counterparts. I traded nods with them and the other folks walking by.

I finished my drink and was thinking about ordering another. But then, a voice caught my attention.

"Having fun?" Someone asked.

I looked up at a woman. She was about the same age as me: brunette, with gold earrings, a dark pantsuit, and an aura of polished poise. I couldn't see her name tag.

I smiled shyly and shrugged. "Sure. Something like that."

She tilted her head and smiled. "What do you mean by that?"

"Hmm." I searched for my words. "I guess I don't see the point... Of networking events. Or, networking in general. I'm only here because my HR head suggested it."

"You don't think much of networking?" The woman chuckled a bit. "You mean you've never needed advice or help from someone?"

"Well, that's not really networking," I said. "Networking is more like... a sales pitch. And I'd rather leave that to my sales staff."

"Tell you what," the woman said. She pointed to two people about fifteen feet away. "Those two are friends of mine. The man's name is Stephen Shedletzky, and the woman is Susan Gregory. If you don't believe in networking after talking to them, I'll admit that it's pointless."

"Really?" I asked.

"Really."

I took another look at the two.

Stephen seemed like one of those people that perpetually smiled. He had curly dark brown hair that dipped into a sharp widow's peak. He was dressed in dark jeans and a blazer—slightly more casual than the power-suits around him.

Susan was a brunette, wearing a turquoise blouse with a navy pin-striped skirt. She spoke with an accent that I placed somewhere between British and New Zealand.

Susan and Stephen were different from everyone else in the room. I could see it from how they stood, how they spoke, and how they smiled. They looked like they were actually having fun *and* connecting with people.

What did I have to lose?

"I think I'll do that. Thanks," I said. I put down my glass by the table, pushed off from the bar, and approached the two.

"Excuse me?" I asked. They turned to look at me. "Um, there was a woman over there who—oh, that's strange. She's vanished."

"Ah, I think we know who you're talking about." Susan said with a laugh. "Sorry—I didn't catch your name?"

"Russell. Russell Baxter," I said, extending my hand. "At any rate, that woman suggested I ask you both about networking."

"Oh, really?" Stephen grinned. "Well, that is something we like to talk about."

"So. Russell." Susan gestured to the room. "You came to meet a whole lot of people, right?"

"I guess?" I said.

Stephen put his hand on my back.

"Sell yourself?" He asked.

"Probably?"

"Make money?" Susan held out her thumb and forefinger and rubbed them together.

"In the long run." I agreed.

"Okay," Stephen said. He took his arm away. "If you want to network effectively, stop doing those things. Now."

There was a moment of silence.

"Are you still doing it?" Stephen asked.

"What? No." I said.

"Good." Susan said. "You see, networking isn't about just making money, or making a ton of connections."

"It's a lot more about finding people whose values and beliefs align with yours." Stephen continued. "That way, you can combine your strengths and work towards a common goal together."

"Okay," I nodded slowly, not quite buying it. "That sounds good and all, but it's not exactly going to get my company the results we need. I'm not in this for fun. I'm in it for Prism."

I reached into my pocket and pulled out my own stack of cards. There were a hundred of them, bound by a blue rubber band.

I held out the cards to Stephen and Susan. "I need to find someone to help us with a customer service initiative. I have one hundred cards. That means if I spread out as many cards as possible, I'll have more chances of finding what I need than if I spend my time finding one person whose values align with mine."

Stephen whistled.

"Fancy cards," Susan said. "Could I see them?"

I handed her the stack. She looped off the rubber band and leafed through them. "Wow. That is a lot of them."

"Pity you don't need them." Stephen said.

"... What?" I asked.

"Look." Stephen pointed out across the room. "Your machine-gun philosophy is going to turn you into her."

I followed Stephen's eyes, and saw a familiar character. Donna Jones: the woman with the card-stuffed name tag. She was back, still trying to impose her software on bystanders.

"Excuse me," she barreled into a circle of people, knocking a smaller man out of her way. "Excuse me. Do any of you want to boost your sales? Because our software uses two different levels of—"

"She's what I call a Pez Dispenser." Stephen said. "On auto-pilot, firing out business cards. And I guarantee you, she's not going to create loyalty with behavior like that. She'll fail more often, work harder without getting any more results, and give up once she hits her target. Spaghetti against the wall."

I grunted. Stephen had a point.

Susan added. "Somewhere down the line, we made networking

something it isn't supposed to be. It's not about selling yourself to as many people as possible."

"Instead, it's about building meaningful connections with people." Stephen continued. "People who believe the same things as you, who share the same vision for the future. People who are driven by a common purpose."

"And then putting effort into building those relationships, so both parties can benefit." Susan said. "Not so you can just get something out of them."

I was still staring at Donna, the Pez Dispenser. She'd gotten a few sheepish people to take her business cards. I doubted they'd be calling her back.

"Alright," I said. "So, let's say I believe you. How do I network tonight?"

"That's easy," Stephen said. "Find people with the same values and beliefs as you, and combine your strengths with theirs to accomplish your shared purpose. An easy way to do that is to strike up a conversation with people, share what's important to you, and if you get a positive emotional response from them—bam—you're compatible."

"My values?" I asked. "Like, family? Democracy? Long live the Queen?"

Susan stifled a giggle. "What are you trying to accomplish with your company?"

"Well Nancy, our HR head, said I could find someone to help with our customer service—" I began.

"No, no," she waved her hands. "I mean—what are you up to at your company, as a whole? What's your purpose?"

I thought about it.

"... Selling toasters?" I ventured. "And other low-energy kitchen appliances."

"Russell. You could do anything in the world. Why Prism?"

Why Prism indeed? I crossed my arms and thought about it.

"Because I love the company." I said. "The people in it are like family. And I also love our mission—to make our world more sustainable with low-energy products, and to deliver something valuable to our customers."

Stephen nodded encouragingly. "I suggest you lead with that."

And I did start with that—our mission. From end to end, I worked my way across the room. I shook hands, had a drink, and told some jokes. And do you know what?

Turns out I didn't like most of the people in that room. However, that didn't end up being a bad thing. If I'd done my rapid-fire plan, I could have ended up working with someone I couldn't stand.

There was one exception though.

As the activity in the Rose Suite settled down, I tucked myself away in a corner. I'd taken out my name tag, and was writing a few notes on it.

"Ugh." I shook my pen and scribbled; I was running out of ink.

That's when I felt a presence behind me.

"Hi, Russell. I spoke to Stephen and Susan." A woman's voice said. "They seemed pretty pleased to meet you."

I turned. It was the woman again—the brunette woman by the bar. I still couldn't see her name tag.

"Yes." I said. "Well, it went both ways! They were great people. I'm sorry. I don't even get your name."

"It's Cindy Stradling," she said. "And I might just be able to—wait, what are you doing?"

I glanced at my name tag, and the half-finished notes.

"I'm actually writing down all the insights Stephen and Susan shared with me." I said. "But my pen's out of ink."

Cindy smirked. She handed me a pen. On the pen were the words *Athena Training and Consulting Inc.*.

"Thanks." I said. I put the pen in my pocket and resolved to finish my notes later. "Anyway, yes—I learned a lot. You said your name was Cindy?"

"Yes," she said. "And from what Stephen and Susan shared with me, I'd like to speak to you some more myself."

Cindy and I had an interesting conversation after that. We talked about ourselves and what's important to us. We discussed my career, and what was going on at Prism. And we talked a bit about her company: Athena Training and Consulting Inc..

I left the networking event feeling like I'd actually done something. I'd met three intriguing, genuine people. And, when I got back home, I even had a pen to finish my notes on what I'd learned.

NOTES FROM RUSSELL'S NAME TAG

WHAT NETWORKING ISN'T

Networking isn't selling a product, or selling yourself. It's not an excuse to get your name out there to as many folks as possible. It's not an excuse to be sleazy. It's not an attempt to take advantage of others, or to have others take advantage of you. Networking IS NOT being a Pez Dispenser that gives away business cards that no one asks for.

WHAT NETWORKING SHOULD BE

Networking is the act of making genuine connections and fostering the connections you choose for the long-term. It starts by finding out your own values and purpose, and then finding other people with similar ones—people who believe what you believe.

WHAT STEPS TO TAKE

Start by realizing who you are. What is the core of your mission? What goals are you trying to achieve in your organization and career? When we talk about "goals," we don't mean goals like "making a sale" or "becoming VP." We mean more substantial goals that contribute towards a vision of the world, and how it could be better.

Thought leader Simon Sinek says, "People don't buy what you do. They buy why you do it." Share your purpose first instead of your product. This will get you more meaningful responses, and will help differentiate you from the crowd. "My name is Russell Baxter and I sell toasters," won't find you the same meaningful connections as "my name is Russell Baxter. I believe that industry can work together with the environment, and we do so by empowering people to make smart decisions about their kitchen appliances." People who believe what you believe will be fascinated by what you do.

Try to make a few valuable connections. They're much more sustainable and useful than short-term professional flings. And you don't have to limit your connections to networking events either. You can build your network by meeting with your trusted colleagues one-on-one, and asking them for people who align with your beliefs.

Play the long game! Networking isn't about getting quick results from people—that's just manipulation. Instead, it's about benefiting from collaboration and mutual interest over a long period of time. As leaders, we have a clear understanding of our values and an ability to articulate a vision of the future that we are contributing towards. Leaders know that they cannot do it alone. Networking is one way to grow our following and tribe as leaders.

BLIND SPOT TWO
Leading Without a Personal Brand

Russell wrapped up his story. "A lot of things changed for me after that night."

"Cindy?" Amir asked. "That name sounds familiar."

"It should," Russell said. "I just got off the phone with her when you came to see me."

"You're still in touch?"

Russell nodded. "Oh yes. Cindy is a professional trainer, and we've known each other for years now. She's the founder of Athena Training and Consulting Inc., and the Athena Alliance, a group of top international trainers and coaches. After I met her at that networking event, I was intrigued with her, and the collective knowledge her alliance could offer. In fact, I turned out to need that knowledge for a problem that came up that Monday."

★

The Monday following my networking night, I drove to work as usual. I had no idea that meeting Cindy and her friends last Friday would fundamentally change my professional life. I also had no idea that I'd need her help so soon.

By half-past eight, I'd navigated through the rush hour traffic and arrived at our office.

I pulled into the lot, and parked my Saturn in my reserved space, which was right next to the doors. I hitched my briefcase strap over my shoulder, stepped out of my car, and tossed my coffee cup into a nearby garbage can.

I was about to push through the doors and enter the building, when I turned back to look at my car.

Although I definitely liked the convenience of the spot, I still hadn't gotten used to it being so *visible*.

My car sat right at the front of the lot—in the very first space, closest to the building. Every person walking into work—whether they were from Prism, or from one of the other offices—could see exactly when I was in the office, and exactly when I wasn't. It was a big change from when I joined the company.

Ten years ago, when I started at Prism, I parked at the far end of the parking lot. Back then I was a behind-the-scenes data gatherer, ad-planner and copy-pitching machine. I put in some long hours, but I loved marketing, and I loved the company. Ten years later, I was head of the marketing department—leading a team and doing work that I found exciting and rewarding. All the effort and long hours paid off; I was awarded the CEO position when Tim decided to move on.

During that time, I'd gotten to know a lot about Prism: its staff, its strategies, its mission. But, as I stared at my new parking space, I wondered, how much did I know about Russell the CEO? And how much did he really know about leading a company?

"Hi Russell."

I straightened up and spun around. Nancy Saunders tilted her head and smiled.

Back then, Nancy was the head of Human Resources, and probably my best friend in the whole company.

"Hi there, Nancy." I straightened my tie. "How was your weekend?"

"Not bad." Nancy shrugged. She held the door open for me. "Did you end up going to that networking night?"

"I did! And I met some interesting people." I said. "Thanks for suggesting it."

Nancy and I rode the elevator up, and I filled her in on the networking event—and the people I'd met there. When the elevator opened on our floor, Nancy reminded me of a meeting that afternoon, and we went our separate ways.

I dropped my briefcase off in my office, and spent some time looking at emails. A few minutes past nine, Larissa knocked on my door.

Larissa was my assistant: a young woman who'd graduated from Humber the year before. She held a yellow file folder tucked underneath her arm.

"Morning Russell, how'd your weekend go?" She asked.

"Very nice, thanks." I said. "What's this folder?"

"It's a Tim file." She said. She handed it to me. "Those sales projections you wanted."

Tim Kellerman was our last CEO, a big man with a big voice, a big car, and a fondness for flashy, expensive ties. He'd left Prism two months ago to manage a telecommunications company, but some of the tasks he'd been overseeing still needed to be wrapped up.

I thanked Larissa and leafed through the yellow folder. It was filled with sales projections for the next three months.

As I looked through the numbers folder, I found something I hadn't noticed before. I picked up the office phone and dialed the extension for Craig, our sales manager.

"Hi Craig, quick question." I said, looking through a few pages from the folder. "I'm looking at the sales projections that Tim did before he left, and I was sure we could sell more than this. In fact, the last time I looked at the numbers, I thought we could easily increase our client base by at least ten percent just by selling to a broader base of retailers. Why haven't we had our sales team focus on that?"

"Well, I can come up and look over the file." Craig said. "But Tim always thought we should focus on selling to core markets, the hardware stores and niche shops—that's where the money's always been."

"But…" I said. "That made sense when we were new, but now we're established, and energy efficiency is right in the public eye."

"Well," Craig said. "I guess we can start thinking about building our client base to the mainstream retailers."

I bit my lip and thought about it. If we did make an aggressive push into increasing our territory, this company could soar. On the other hand, our sales staff were experts at locking down deals with places like Home Depot and Rona. And, if we diverted the sales staff's attention from our core customers, we might just give more room for our competition to gain a foothold. What if my ideas were wrong, and we didn't sign any new clients? I'd have sent our sales team on a wild goose chase, without bringing any additional benefits to the company.

"Um, no." I said. I closed the folder. "I guess if Tim thought it was a good plan—I shouldn't shake things up too much. Especially since I just came in."

I hung up the phone, and shut the folder, feeling frustrated for some reason. I decided to go get a coffee. On the way, I passed Gary Aviv's cubicle, and remembered something.

I said. "Gary, I want to move Carrie next to the HR people for a while. Can you make it happen?"

"I dunno." Gary said. "Tim thought it was a pretty good idea for her to be next to the finance guys…"

"He did?" I asked. I leaned my elbows on his cubicle wall. "But, don't you think, since HR is drafting their new policy papers for manufacturing, it'd be beneficial for them to be near our only technical writer? Carrie doesn't do any work with finance."

"It's your call." Gary shrugged. "But Tim thought it was a really good idea."

I chewed my lip. "Fine." I said. "We'll keep her there for now."

I resumed my trip to the kitchen. I came across Susanne—one of the marketing staff—as she came out with a mug of tea.

"Hey Susanne, can I get a meeting with you later about that ad space?" I asked.

"Sure thing, Tim." She said.

I froze. I looked back at Suzanne. She kept walking calmly down the hall; she hadn't even noticed the mistake.

I didn't bother getting coffee after all. Instead, I walked back to my office. When I got there, I shut the door behind me and collapsed into my chair.

I rubbed my temples. I knew I was good at my job. I knew that I was a good leader. If I wasn't, then I wouldn't have been named CEO when Tim had left. So, why did I feel so unsure of myself? And why did it feel like Tim Kellerman was still running the show? I was behaving like he was still giving orders. In fact, I was allowing myself to live in his shadow.

I tapped my pen, and realized it was the one Cindy had given me at the networking event—the one with ATHENA TRAINING AND CONSULTING INC. written on it.

I turned up the pen. There was a phone number on the side. I flipped open my cell and dialed the number.

"Cindy Stradling? Hi. This is Russell Baxter."

"Russell, from the Hemisphere Hotel?" Cindy asked. "What a surprise!"

We spent a minute catching up, talking about the event, and our weekends, when I launched into what was on my mind.

"Actually Cindy, I was so impressed with you on Friday, that I thought I'd reach out for some professional advice. Do you have a minute to talk?"

I began to tell her about my morning, and how I was still deferring to Tim.

"This is the way it has been since I have stepped into my new role." I said. "I follow what the old CEO would do, even when it goes against my instincts, and the direction I want to take the company in. When I bring up a new idea to my staff, they continually remind me of what Tim believed or did. And because I don't want to make the wrong move I go along with it. Frankly, I feel like I'm selling out, and for the first time I feel confused about who I am."

"Well it can be a real challenge to follow in the footsteps of a leader that was liked." Cindy said.

"Thanks." I said. "But regardless: I want to run this company based on my experience and successes. And I want to feel good about my leadership and my decisions."

Cindy told me she knew the perfect person for the job: an executive coach in the Athena Alliance named Dorothy Lazovik.

Cindy gave me Dorothy's phone number, which I wrote down on a Post-it. I said goodbye to Cindy, put down the phone, and moved to go get Larissa. But then, I stopped myself.

I was going to tell Larissa to call Dorothy, and set up some time to talk, but did I really want Larissa calling Dorothy? What if everyone found out I was looking for coaching?

It wouldn't look good, I decided. Tim had never needed any training, at least, not that I knew of.

I crumbled the paper into a ball. I'd call Dorothy myself.

I dialed Dorothy's number. She answered on the second ring.

"Good morning, Dorothy Lazovik."

I introduced myself. I told her that Cindy had directed me to her, and that I was hoping to learn more about her coaching.

In a few minutes, Dorothy immediately put me at ease. She assured me that I wasn't the only new leader to feel uncertain of how to take command in a new role. She asked me a few questions, and pointed out a few things that I was doing right. It was a valuable conversation, and it felt good to talk to someone without being judged.

I decided I wanted to learn more about Dorothy, and what she could offer in terms of coaching. We agreed to meet on Wednesday, at the hotel close to our offices for a coffee in their restaurant.

That Wednesday, just before lunch, I quietly excused myself from a conversation with Nancy. I went back to my office, threw on my coat, and headed out to my car. I got in, and drove to the Atrium hotel.

The Atrium hotel and corporate center was a big stucco building inspired by Spanish villas. They served travelers from the airport. The restaurant where I was supposed to meet Dorothy was off to the side of the building.

I found a parking space just in time to avoid being late for my meeting. I ran up to the café and pushed the double-doors open. The café interior was dark hardwood, with some abstract art up for sale on the walls.

The café was mostly empty. I looked around, and spotted someone at the corner of the room. She looked just like her picture on her website: short dark hair, a big smile and professionally dressed.

I approached her. "Excuse me, you must be Dorothy Lazovik."

The woman beamed. "Indeed I am. And you must be Russell. It's a pleasure to meet you."

"Likewise," I said. She stood up to shake my hand. Dorothy had a firm handshake and a warm smile. "Thanks very much for seeing me on such short notice."

"My pleasure. I'm glad I was able to accommodate you." Dorothy said.

While we waited for our coffee, we spoke casually about family and interests. I wanted to know a bit more about Dorothy's background, and found that she wasn't just a coach: she was also a workshop facilitator, a keynote speaker, and passionate advocate for mentoring young female professionals.

Then the conversation turned to business and Dorothy began to ask me about my career and the challenges I was facing. She had some questions that I hadn't even given thought to before: not just asking what I wanted to achieve, but how those achievements would affect me and my role as a leader. We discussed my career, my goals at Prism, and the challenges I'd been facing lately with my own identity. I ended up summarizing my feelings that I discussed with her on Monday.

"I want to run the company according to my vision." I said. "But I feel like I'm not respected, or seen as the leader just yet. Instead, everyone defaults to Tim's old plans and opinions. Tim was smart, but I see this company going in a new direction if we want to grow."

Dorothy listened intently. Occasionally, she made notes on a pad of paper. When I finished talking, she put her pen down and looked me in the eye.

"Well Russell, what you are telling me sounds quite normal: it's typical for new leaders to jump into their roles, and start working on the business needs instead of taking the time to establish a clear vision that inspires their employees to follow them." She said.

I breathed a sigh of relief. It was good to know that I wasn't the only one who felt like this.

Dorothy continued. "But, now that you've been in your role for a few months, you're really ready to take the lead: you'll need to create a vision for Prism, and where it's going. You'll need to do more than just illustrate your plans, you'll have to inspire people with its confidence and clarity. To get that confidence and clarity, you need to define your personal brand."

"Personal brand." I repeated. "I saw the term on your website, and Cindy mentioned it, but I'd like to get a clearer idea of what exactly it entails."

Our coffee arrived. Dorothy had ordered a regular coffee, and I'd ordered a Turkish coffee, just to see what it looked like. The Turkish coffee came in a small glass flute, with dark brown sludge lurking on the bottom.

Dorothy poured some cream into her coffee, and stirred.

"Well, you're familiar with product branding?" Dorothy asked.

"I hope so," I joked. "I led the marketing department for a decade after all: a brand is essentially a reputation. For instance, when I went to a Nordstrom's with my wife to get a pair of shoes, we experienced the best customer service ever. My wife was ecstatic with the experience, and shared it with everyone. My wife's story—combined with the stories that others tell of Nordstrom's amazing customer service—form the brand that's made their store famous."

"Exactly. And just as products and stores have brands" Dorothy said, "So do people. Your brand is the reputation that you build up from your interactions with others. When people have a good experience with you, it creates a story that influences your own personal brand."

I nodded to show that I was getting it. Dorothy continued. "We all have personal brands, so it makes sense to invest some time to consider how you want to be known so you can accurately establish the impression you make with others. A leader whose brand shows uncertainty and hesitation will not inspire others to follow. On the other hand, a leader with a brand that's confident, passionate and genuine *will* get people to buy-in to their ideas."

In the corner of my eye, I noticed a shape out the window. It was a truck, pulling a trailer on the road. The sides of the trailer bore an ad for Levi's jeans. It was interesting to think that both me, and the jeans, had our own brand.

I rest my elbows on the table, and propped up my chin.

What Dorothy was saying made sense, but I wasn't used to thinking about myself like this. I'd come in just looking for advice on how to lead with authority, but now she was suggesting that I needed to work on myself first before I could direct others. It was a lot more holistic than I thought it'd be.

"So, before I lead others, I'll need to work on myself." I said. "I'll need to establish a powerful, authentic brand that will help me share my vision with a conviction that'll inspire others to follow me. Is that more or less it?"

"There are some more details that are involved, though you're getting it." Dorothy said.

"So how do I start establishing my personal brand?" I asked. "How do I inspire people as Russell Baxter?"

Dorothy said. "Well, this all starts with defining who you are, what your strengths are, and knowing how you want others to be talking about you."

I thought about it. "I'm not quite certain how to answer that."

Dorothy leaned forward a bit. "Well Russell, before we do anything else, I'd like you to think about how you want to be known as a leader."

I looked into the Turkish coffee, and pondered Dorothy's words.

"Well." I began. "I think... I'm big believer in people, and what they can do. I believe our business isn't powered by our technology—which was what Tim thought—but by the talent in the office. And I think Prism will only grow once we begin to tap into our talent pool."

"Your people-centered vision will be a powerful one to share, but it's not where we need to start." Dorothy pressed on. "Right now, we need to focus on you, not Prism, on how you want to be seen, not how you *don't* want to be seen."

I took a sip of the coffee. It was good. Maybe it was the tingle of the caffeine, but I felt more ideas about myself come up.

"Okay, I think I have it." I held up my finger. "I want people to know me as a fair, honest, and authentic leader. I want them to know I'm passionate about growing talent, and that I'm approachable. I want them to know that I'm apolitical, that I value innovation, and that I'll always do my best to do right by my staff, and by our customers. And yes, I'd like to be confident and inspiring when I need to be."

"Wow, Russell!" Dorothy said. "That's quite a description you have for yourself."

"Shucks," I said. "I just had to think about it. But knowing how I want to be seen, how can I create that image for myself?"

"A personal brand starts with how you are known." Dorothy said. "So, we will work together to get clear on the perceptions you want to create in the minds of others, and the behaviours you'll need to demonstrate to bring them to life. From there, we'll get clear on what is important to you, address your mindset to reduce any resistance and self-doubt that's keeping you from being confident in your role as CEO."

I rubbed my chin and thought about it. Stephen and Susan had already told me the value of connecting with people by knowing your core beliefs and values. Was this the logical next step to that belief? I went over the experience with Dorothy, highlighting the connection between the two.

Dorothy nodded. "Leaders lead best when they speak and act in a way that aligns with who they really are. When you know your values, passions, key strengths and natural talents, and act on them consistently, you build equity in your brand, and establish what others can expect from you, every time. When you combine that with authentic leadership, and communicating your ideas, you'll be respected, and the comparison between you and Tim will naturally fall away, because you'll be a genuine Russell, instead of a second-rate Tim."

Dorothy paused for emphasis. "And when employees experience a leader being authentic, knowing what they want, and sharing a vision that matters, they trust them and are more willing to follow them."

"It sounds like a long journey though." I murmured. "How would we start?"

Dorothy moved her mug to the side and clasped her hands together. "It all starts with a decision to want to change and do the work to make that change happen. You have to be clear on *what you want*. You need to think about *who you need to be* to achieve that. And finally, you have to know *the things you need to do* to get there."

I tapped my fingers on the table, and thought. This wasn't a way of thinking that I was used to—but then again—the challenges that I would face as CEO were something entirely new as well. I needed to be at my best: not just for myself, but for the company.

"Let's do it." I said. "I know what I want, and who I need to be. But there's the question again—how do we start?"

"With a plan and a lot of practice." Dorothy said. "If we work together, we can build the framework for your brand, which will provide you with a guideline to follow to ensure that you consistently perform in alignment with who you are to create the results you want."

I suddenly realized that I should write this down. I patted my pants for a piece of paper and a pen. All I came up with was my Blackberry.

"I need to get a notepad." I whispered, texting a note to myself.

NOTES FROM RUSSELL'S BLACKBERRY

WHAT PERSONAL BRANDING IS, AND WHY IT'S IMPORTANT

A personal brand is, essentially, your reputation as determined by the experience you create for the people around you. Your brand affects how people approach you, think about you, and even how they match you up for work.

We all have a brand. It's the sum of our actions—big and small. From how you do your job, to how you dress, it all paints a picture that other people will use to create their idea of you, and the story they share.

It's easy to forget that our brand exists. And it's even easier to forget that we can directly influence our personal brand. By being conscious of our brand, and by acting with intent, we can be strategic about building the brand we want.

If you've ever been passed over for a promotion, or if you've ever felt disrespected, it's a good time to check in on your personal brand, seek feedback from others, and discover what you are doing to contribute to that, and work to align your brand to become an authentic reflection of you.

COMMON MISUNDERSTANDINGS IN PERSONAL BRANDING

The biggest misunderstanding that people face is the difference between who they are, and who they think they should be. Often, we act in a way we think our role requires—even if it's not really us.

It's a mistake to think your title requires you to act in a certain way. You are not your title: it is an external label that does not dictate who you are. Instead, master who you are, and be that.

Ask yourself—who am I? Really? What drives my decisions? How do I want to be known? Knowing these answers is a great place to start building the brand you want.

HOW TO BE INTENTIONAL IN CREATING YOUR PERSONAL BRAND

You are in control of the experiences you create. And, as such, it is important to step up and be deliberate in shaping your brand.

Start by defining a vision of what you want, who you are, and how you want to be perceived. From there, align your behavior to reflect the perception you want to create, and make adjustments when your behavior doesn't align with your brand. Consider the following tools that shape your brand:

Words. Your language carries energy, and reveals how you feel about yourself. Strong decisive leaders use positive words, speak with purpose, and don't use fillers like ums and ahs and winding sentences. Transparent, authentic leaders share information and take full accountability for their choices.

Actions. When you have defined who you want to be, and what keywords exemplify your brand, it's time to bring those words to life with action. In other words: you need to walk your talk. When you commit to, say, being an approachable, patient CEO, you don't want to brush people off, or respond gruffly when you speak to others—and if you're passionate about an issue, you need to get involved and support it.

The experience you create. Walking your talk. The way you dress. The energy you project. Your conversations, whether you are gossiping or sharing a win you and your team have accomplished. Everything you do and say, especially as you climb higher in the ranks, is being evaluated more closely. People make judgments based on snap shots of you. These can all subtly influence the way people view you, and all influence the path you can take in an organization.

BLIND SPOT THREE
Neglecting to Develop Your Direct Managers

The Monday after my first personal branding lesson with Dorothy, I came across Nancy in the hall.

"Hi Russell," Nancy said. "Nice vest."

"Thanks." I looked down at it. My wife said sweater-vests made me look dweeby, but I thought they were cool. The vest was a small but poignant affirmation of what Dorothy had talked to me about. As a clothing choice, it wasn't very Tim, but it screamed of Russell.

"Where are you coming from?" I asked, smoothing out the vest.

"An exit interview," Nancy said. "Ali just left."

"Ali is gone?" I gasped. "He was our top network specialist!"

"It is a loss." Nancy admitted.

"Indeed," I said. We fell in step together. "And he was such a pleasure to work with. I guess I expected him to always be around."

"Actually," Nancy said. "I get the feeling that he would have stayed. Except..."

I quirked my eyebrow. "Tony?"

"Tony." Nancy confirmed.

Tony was the manager for our IT department. A compact man with a wiry frame and a bristling black moustache, Tony was a tightly-wrapped package of energy, big dreams, and a little arrogance. He also worked as a project manager when we needed software for our products, and made a few sales with some fringe distributors. It was an unusual position, but he'd been here since the beginning of the company, when there were too many projects and not enough people. When I first joined Prism, Tony was already a veteran.

Athena Alliance Members

The old CEO, Tim, never had any problems with Tony. They'd been grand chums. But back when I was still coming up as a project manager in marketing, I remember disagreeing with Tony's leadership policies. I could live with his irregular emails and sometimes schizophrenic approach to problem-solving, but what really rattled me was the way he treated his staff.

Ali wasn't the first to cite Tony as a reason for leaving. In the past two years, three IT staff had left, claiming that they just couldn't get along with him. I found that worrisome.

"I'm going to have to… explore this with Tony a bit." I said. I veered away from Nancy.

The IT department was a small cluster of computers at the end of our floor. Cardboard boxes of wires, software, and presentation handouts created a tiny town around the desks.

Tony had an office just to the left of the cubicles. The door was open. I peered inside.

Tony was in. And so was Carrie, the technical writer.

"I'm pretty sure you told me the tickets were supposed to be written up according to the form in our ongoing folder," Carrie said. She had a stack of papers hugged to her chest.

"That's crazy!" Tony waved a hand. "I wouldn't say something like that."

"Well then." Carrie took out a sheaf of paper from her stack. "Could you tell me which format you'd like now so we don't run into this problem again? I've been trying to—"

"Ask Debra." Tony interrupted.

"But if you just tell me which form you'd like to use now—" Carrie began, but Tony had noticed me waiting.

"Ah, Russell! Hello, hello." Tony waved me in. "Just showing Carrie the ropes. She still has a bit to learn right? You can go, Carrie."

Carrie nodded slowly. I thought I heard her scream inside her head. I watched her leave the office. She had the air of someone living in constant frustration.

"Tony?" I asked. "I came down here because—"

"Oh, one second." Tony held out a finger. "I'm buzzing."

Tony whipped out his Blackberry. His brow furrowed. "Another ticket? Excuse me for a second Russell."

I watched as Tony typed out an email on his phone. I realized I was staring with my mouth open. I shut it.

"Aaand send." Tony clicked the ENTER button on his phone and tucked it back into his belt clip. "What was it you wanted to talk about?"

I set my lips into a line.

"I want to talk about Ali." I said. "He just left his exit interview. There was… talk that direct management in the IT department contributed to him leaving."

Tony looked honestly shocked. "Well. I don't know anything about that."

"Are you sure about that?" I asked. I gave a sidelong glance to the door Carrie just left through. Tony's face remained blank.

I had a sudden thought.

"Tony, I know you've been here a while, but have you ever read anything about managing people?" I asked. "Taken courses? A seminar maybe?"

Tony shrugged. "Nope." He said, happily. "Picked it up as I went along. Same with you, eh?"

"Not quite," I muttered. "Tony, ever since I started advancing, I've been reading books, taking seminars, and getting coaching."

Tony just shrugged.

A few months ago, I might have just mumbled something and walked away. But after training with Dorothy, I wasn't intimidated. I looked up at Tony.

"Tony, I'd like to follow up with you on this later." I said. "In the meantime, I have to take care of something."

I headed back to my office feeling frustrated.

I had two major concerns. Firstly, Tony hadn't realized that his behavior could have caused Ali to leave. Secondly, I don't even think Tony cared that a top performer had left.

I reached my office and plunked into my chair. I had to run over the progress of the product development team, but instead, I folded my hands under my chin, and thought.

This wasn't the first time a valuable employee had left because of dysfunctional leadership. Across the board, it sometimes felt were running a race to retain our top talent. Losing Ali was a red flag for a very widespread problem.

But maybe it didn't have to be like this. Maybe our mid-level managers could learn the tools to attract and engage top talent, instead of repelling them.

I decided to get a coffee.

I headed for the kitchen. On the way I saw Austin Schwartz, our head finance guy, walking by with his nose buried in a large manila folder. Austin managed two accountants, two analysts, and a lawyer.

"Austin." I said, stopping him. "I'm toying with an idea here and would like your input; what would you think of a program to boost your leadership abilities along with the other leaders at Prism?"

"Interesting. I think it'd be very valuable." Austin said. He dropped the folder to his side. "I do my best, but after four years of this position, it's still been tough guiding people."

I nodded, and continued on my way to the kitchen. As I stepped through the door, I bumped into Rohit Binder. Rohit was the leader of marketing—my old department. I asked Rohit the same question I'd posed Austin.

"Absolutely," he admitted. "I read books on my own. But I've always thought a more integrated approach would help."

I thanked Rohit and went in the kitchen to pour myself a mug of rich, black sludge from the coffee maker. I took a tentative sip.

Now knowing what motor oil must taste like, I dumped the evil beverage in the sink and headed back to my office. I picked up the phone, and dialed a number. "Hi Cindy. This is Russell. I have a doozy of a situation for you."

I explained my situation to Cindy, from Ali's exit interview, to Tony's lack of concern.

"But it's not just Tony." I continued. "While my other direct managers have good intentions, they all feel they could improve their leadership skills. Frankly, it's pretty surprising."

"Well Russell, have you invested in your middle managers before?" Cindy asked me.

"Now that I think about it, no." I answered. "I guess it's not that much of a surprise after all. Anyway, do you think you have anyone who could help?"

"I actually have the perfect person for the job." Cindy said. "Her name is Julie Ruben Rodney, and I can connect you with her right away."

Cindy explained. Julie Ruben Rodney was another member of the Athena Alliance. Julie managed her own company that delivered leadership development sessions in multiple learning formats. She sounded perfect. If Cindy was right, her style would fit perfectly with the culture here.

After my talk with Cindy, I called up Julie and asked if she could meet to discuss our needs.

Julie and I traded emails and phone calls for a few weeks, and met up a few times to discuss the investment I wanted to make in my direct managers. About a month after I first called Cindy, I sent out an email to all of my direct managers: there was a program kicking off next week, and they were all invited.

That Monday, I walked in early into the boardroom where our first facilitated session was about to take place. A young woman with black hair was peering over a projector, tweaking the resolution. I knocked on the open door.

"Hi there, Julie." I said. "Nice to see you again! I can't wait to put this program into action."

Julie stood up, brushed her hair back, and smiled. She returned my handshake. "Likewise, Russell! I hope everyone's ready for our leadership journey."

"Oh, I know they are." I said. "They should start filtering in any minute now."

I left Julie to her work and took a seat near the back of the room. I was joined by Nancy five minutes later. Bit by bit, the conference room filled up with Prism's direct managers.

When we were at capacity, Julie walked to the front of the room. She walked around, met people, and introduced herself. After getting a feel for the room, Julie took her place at the head of the projector. She surveyed the room. When she had everyone's attention, she began.

"Do you know what the biggest strength of this company is?" Julie asked.

"Superior products?" Austin Schwartz ventured.

"A powerful sales process?" Rohit suggested.

"A spectacular IT infrastructure!" Tony exclaimed. This drew a few chuckles.

Julie chuckled with them. "All good answers," she said. "But I'm going to say that the biggest strength of this company is its employees. Specifically, engaged employees."

Julie began to pace slowly around the front of the room.

"More engaged employees generate more profit." Julie said. "It sounds like a wishy-washy thing, but it's true."

She clicked the remote to the projector. A slide popped up on the screen. It showed an overview of an engagement study, and a simplified chart. Company profitability was measured with orange bars, and employee engagement was measured with yellow ones. As the yellow bars lengthened, so did the orange ones.

"Metrics show that when employees are more engaged, the company succeeds." Julie said. "And do you know how we engage employees?"

Julie held out her hands. "Anyone?"

"Good pay?" Someone opined.

"Perks? Like flex-time?"

"Well-designed software!" Tony added. No one chuckled this time.

Julie smirked. "Actually, the answer is sitting in front of me. Direct managers. It's the direct managers that can engage or disengage employees."

Austin raised his hand.

"Yes?" Julie asked.

"But Julie," he said. "Don't our promotion and hiring practices downplay this importance? I was promoted for my hard skills, not how good I was at softer skills like engaging people."

"That's exactly it." Julie said. "There's an assumption that if you're good at your technical skills, you'll also be good at leading people. In reality, that's quite rare."

Julie continued. "Most of us got promoted to a leadership position by being very good at our technical jobs. But that doesn't mean necessarily that we have all the tools to lead people. After all, if you ran an airline, and promoted your best pilot to manage all the airline staff, that company probably wouldn't do so well. The two jobs—one technical, the other managerial—require completely different skill-sets."

Julie clicked a new slide, showing different aspects of leadership, and ways of developing them.

"And that's why we need to develop strong leadership skills." Julie said. "To help engage employees to perform their best, and to keep top talent around. When employees leave, very rarely do they leave because of the CEO; they leave because their direct manager isn't engaging them."

I sneaked a glance at Tony. He had his lips pursed in concentration. I breathed a sigh of relief. While Tony wasn't *the* reason for this session, I was glad he was taking it in.

"As direct managers, we all need to be self-aware." Julie said. "We need everyone to take time—time to examine their strengths, and their areas for development, and to develop action plans to grow as leaders and direct managers."

Julie held out her hand. "But, instilling and developing these competencies isn't easy. It's an ongoing process to develop as a leader. That's why I combine a combination of classroom learning, coaching, and extensive self-reflection. It's not the sort of thing anyone could fix right now."

"So for now, we'll talk about feedback." Julie said. "I'll explain structures and systems for seeking feedback, and then explain how we can use that to change our behaviors."

For the next hour, Julie demonstrated exactly that. She framed feedback within the much longer journey that we would have to take to develop as leaders. This included reflection and training in other areas, such as communication, delegation, and motivation.

After the session ended, I sent everyone off, encouraging them to work on what Julie had taught them, and taking action on it.

I approached Julie as she was packing up.

"What did you think Russell?" She asked.

"It was insightful," I said. "And I feel that if we integrate these ideas into our management, we'd see some real improvement. But, as you said, one session is just the beginning to solving our challenges to ensure we reach our full potential."

Julie smiled. "Thank you Russell. It's great to work with a CEO who believes in developing his people. As a CEO myself, I know how difficult it can be. I think we can work together on this."

"Super." I said. "I have a question though: since it's so important to keep on learning, how does someone like you do that?"

"Well, I try to learn everywhere." Julie replied. "But these days, I sometimes think my kids sometimes are the best teachers: they *never* censor their feedback."

I chuckled. "We'll have to book them too sometime. Well, same time next month?"

Julie smirked. "Absolutely. I'm looking forward to hearing how people have applied what they learned in our kick-off session."

RUSSELL'S SESSION NOTES

ENGAGEMENT IS CRUCIAL IN THE WORKPLACE

Engagement is much more than just "something nice" to strive for; it's a vital element for a healthy workplace. Engagement is also a major factor in the success of a business. Studies have shown that the more engaged an employee is, the more profitable the company becomes.

Employees who are engaged will work harder, respond better to change, and will persevere through challenges better than disengaged employees.

DIRECT MANAGERS ARE INSTRUMENTAL IN ENGAGEMENT

Direct managers are on the front lines of engagement. The relationship between a direct manager and his or her team can make an immense difference in retaining top talent: it's very rare that an employee will decide leave or stay with a company because of the CEO; instead, employees usually leave or stay based on their relationship with a direct manager.

Direct managers are in the crucial position of managing the most important part of a company: the talent. That's why companies should invest time and effort into developing their direct managers.

LEADERSHIP DOESN'T DEVELOP BY ITSELF

Currently, managers are hired and promoted based on their technical skills—not on their leadership skills.

However, good leadership doesn't necessarily come out of technical skills; think of what would happen if you put a good baker in charge of a pastry company. Leadership requires a number of different skills, and must be constantly developed. This is the best way to make sure your employees stay engaged, and keep delivering to the company.

BLIND SPOT FOUR
Forgetting the "Customer" in Customer Service

"Morning, Russell."

"Morning, Nancy."

A few months later, I walked into the office that week feeling like things were changing for the better. Our direct managers were working better, I was acting as a stronger leader, and I was also putting to action some ideas that I felt would really expand the company.

It had started when I'd decided to hire more customer service staff. It wasn't a Tim move, but it did have a lot of Russell in it. Prism wasn't going to go anywhere if we just poured money into R&D: now that we'd priced our products competitively, it was time to actually do some business.

But, our current customer service team was swamped. Every day, ringing phones went unanswered, emails were lost, and messages went ignored. After reviewing our current needs, and plans for expansion, I'd determined we'd need ten new hires in our customer service team. Nancy had started a hiring blitz to fill the number.

"How's the new staff doing?" I asked Nancy. "The last few just joined us today right?"

Nancy coughed. "Four of them start today. And the other six joined in the last two weeks. Russell… I think we have a problem."

"How so?" I asked.

"We've set up the new workstations in the old boardroom." Nancy said. "Maybe you should take a look."

The old boardroom was at the edge of our floor. A big, unwieldy room that we'd formerly used for storage. I walked over with Nancy, peeked inside, and gasped.

"There are so many of them!" I said.

"There are ten of them, just what you asked for." Nancy whispered.

Ten new staff members. I peered inside again.

Ten was a good number on paper. It matched up with the numbers I'd run through my head and on my calculator. It also matched up with my gut feeling of what would make the company successful. But seeing ten completely new hires milling around in the old boardroom was a little scary.

They didn't know the company. They didn't know our product. They didn't know our brand. How were we going to get them up to speed? And how were we going to train them without making even more work for our senior staff?

"That's a lot of people. How'd we even get enough workstations for them?" I asked.

"IT is still setting up the phones for the newest hires, but we should have just enough." Nancy said.

"Alright." I put my hands on my temples, and started thinking aloud. "We won't be busy for a while. I guess the senior people can show them the ropes for now, then I'm going to schedule a meeting for all customer service staff at three."

I added, "And I'll need to make a call."

"Damage control?" Nancy asked.

"No." I said. I turned away from Nancy and headed back to my office. I felt something powerful rising inside me.

"Damage control is taking the sting out of something bad." I said. "This is an opportunity for us to be spectacular."

Back in my office, I flipped open my cell phone. "Hello? Cindy? I was wondering if you could connect me with a customer service expert."

Ten minutes, I got a call on my office phone. I picked the phone. "Hello?"

A man's voice answered me. "Hello? Russell Baxter? This is David Boyce. Cindy Stradling told me you had an emergency with your customer service staff."

"You could say that." I sat down and swung around on my chair. "We have some new hires starting today—more than we can integrate with traditional methods. I thought it would be a good idea to introduce them all to the company, and I've arranged a general meeting for them."

"That'll be an interesting step for them." David said.

"That's what I thought. So, my question for you is: what do I tell them?" I asked. "I feel like this could be an opportunity to improve our customer service drastically if we do it right."

And a way to really mess up if we did it wrong—was what I didn't say. I drummed my fingers on my armrest.

"Russell, would you have an hour today?" David asked. "It'd be great if I could meet you and learn about the company, your customers, and what's important to you."

That sounded good to me.

I met David in the foyer half an hour later. He was a little younger than me, with a healthy tan and a strong frame.

"Russell," David said. We shook hands. "Nice to meet you."

"Pleasure's mine." I said. "I'm very interested in powering up our customer service staff. I can't wait to hear your thoughts."

"I can't wait to get started!" David said. "Let's start by talking about your staff. How would you describe their roles?"

"Well," I said. "Truth be told, I don't really know. Normally I leave it up to my service managers to train and define the positions for them."

I tilted my head down the hall. David followed me through the office.

"I see." David said. "And why is that?"

"Customer service sort of manages itself, doesn't it?" I asked. "I mean, if they know our policy, our product line, and how to use the phones, they're good to go."

We came to the old boardroom where the new hires were working. About half of them were standing around Jillian—one of our lifers. She was demonstrating how to use our phone system.

"And what does 'good to go' mean to you?" David asked. He held his hands out to the crowd and grinned. I got the message: that was a lot of people that were not "good to go" just yet.

I put my hand on my chin and rubbed the stubble there. "I guess it means dealing with as many calls as possible."

David didn't say anything. I thought some more, and ventured further. "In fact, now that I think about it, I guess they're sort of out of sight, out of mind. Like—you know when you're driving and you don't check your mirrors?"

David turned away from the door. "I find it interesting that you say they're out of mind, Russell. Because your entire company is a service chain to your customers. Your new service staff happens to live at the very end of that chain. To use a metaphor: your company's customer service and support technologies are the safety line on a boat; your customer service staff is the life preserver that the customer grabs on to. And the entire interconnected system is all geared towards connecting to each customer's need, and solving his or her problem."

"I think you've lost me." I said. I left the doorway and leaned against the wall. David joined me. "I don't serve customers in my job."

"Let's explore it together this way," David said. "What does your company do?"

"Well, we make low-energy kitchen appliances." I said.

"And those kitchen appliances—ultimately—are of great value to their owners." David said. "Your stoves cook their meals at dinner-time. Your microwaves heat their popcorn on movie night. And when they get up in the morning, your coffee-makers get them the caffeine they need to get on top of their day. Your products enrich their lives."

David paused to let it sink in. "It sounds to me like your company is actually all about customer service."

"I see your point." I admitted.

We left the old boardroom and headed towards my office. On the way, David stopped at a whiteboard.

"There's a big picture to your business." David said, gesturing at the whiteboard. "And this picture connects everything your company does."

He picked up a blue marker and drew a circle. Inside that circle, he drew a heart. "The customer is at the heart of that picture. Your customers' voices need to be at the heart of that picture."

I nodded. "And I guess it's easy for us to forget that."

"Indeed." David said. He tapped the board. "I define customer service experiences in three levels. When I survey companies about which of those three levels they provide, I find that they often linger at level one and two."

David sketched a little pyramid. He sectioned it off into thirds.

"The reason they stay at those levels," David said, indicating the bottom of the pyramid, "And never reach the top, is that they forget to include the customer at the centre of their story. Who your customers are, what your customers need, and how your company creates value for the customers, needs to be front and centre in everyone's thinking!"

"And, like you said, it's easy to forget that," David said. He capped the marker and lay it down next to the board. "Let's take these new hires for instance. I'm going to quote thought leader Simon Sinek, and 'Start With Why' by asking, why did you hire these new staff?"

"We wanted to expand." I said, folding my arms. "For the business to improve, we need more clients. More clients mean we need more sales and customer service."

"So your staff was optimal before?" David asked.

"Well no, they were busy all the time." I said. "Everyone was doing their best. But they couldn't always keep pace with the calls, emails, and such."

"And how do you think your current clients felt about that?" David asked. "It's the nature and need of business to focus on new expansion. But, we can't forget our current and most loyal clients in the rush to satisfy new ones."

I hadn't thought about it like that before.

I looked down at my chest and ran through my memory of Prism. Like any company, we'd lost clients before. How many of those clients could we have kept by having better customer service? How many clients had we lost because they simply felt ignored?

"I get it." I said to David. "We haven't had the customer at the centre of our thinking. And customer service isn't just our emergency centre: it's key to our company. But now that we have the manpower to address these issues, what do we do with our customer service team?"

David nodded. "Let me answer that with another question: what do you believe is possible?"

David phrased that question with some weight. I paused, and tried to put together my vision.

"I believe Prism can deliver spectacular service to all of its clients." I said. "I think every time a customer calls us, we can leave them feeling satisfied."

I paused again. "But that would need a real powerhouse of a customer service team. And I don't quite know how to get there."

David grinned. He wiped his words off the whiteboard with his arm. "We'll start today. I'll customize an accelerated learning program for your new staff around four key ingredients that are a foundation for a powerhouse service team. And then, we'll add to that foundation: building the *real-world* situational capability, agility and adaptability your customers need from you."

"But," David continued. He finished erasing, and turned to face me.

"Before we do that, we need you to connect your customer service team to their compelling purpose. At this meeting, we'll do that. And we'll do it by telling your new hires a great story."

"What sort of story?" I asked.

"For that, I have to ask you yet another question." David said. "What do your customers need?"

I stopped myself from saying "low-energy kitchen appliances" and instead asked: "How do you mean?"

"Think about it." David said. "If *you* were calling Prism's customer service, what would you want to happen? What would a successful interaction look like? And how would that success reverberate through the company?"

"Well..." I scratched my chin. "I'd give them a call. I'd like them to be polite and helpful. I'd like the call system to be workable, and I'd like them to address all my problems quickly."

"Okay," David continued. "That's a good start, and I think you can go further. Let's look from the outside-in. From your customer's view, from your customer's home, from your customer's dollar, what would bring your brand promise to life within every call to Prism's customer service? What would make that customer service *legendary*?"

"Legendary service?" I screwed my lips tight. "Okay. Let me start over. If I were calling Prism as a customer... I'd need to speak to a person. Not a script."

I thought some more. David waited patiently.

"I'd need to hear the language and feel the commitment of someone operating from a service mindset," I went on. "I'd want them to own my problem. I wouldn't want to feel like they were just 'trying to help' or just doing their job.' I'd need them to be knowledgeable, inquisitive, skillful, and have the freedom and speed to act in my best interest and the company's. And if I had to call several people, I'd sure like them to have some systems and software so that they could pick up on my problem without me explaining it again and again."

I wrapped it up. "And, I'd like them to do it with the warmth, comfort and resolve our customers ask for. That would be legendary service."

"And if your customer service offered you that?" David asked.

"As a customer, I'd keep coming back to them." I said.

I felt like I'd just realized something important. David seemed to read it from my face, and patted me on the shoulder.

"When we start training, I suggest you tell that story to the new hires." David said. "Tell them the story of how a phone call can become a relationship. Tell the story of how that relationship creates real value for the customer, and the company. And when you're done, tell them you believe that that story is true: it's the story of this company from now on. Your staff are the characters that will use their service capability to create spectacular customer experiences that will drive this business. That way, your service stories will become legends. *Legendary*—get it?"

"I've got to write this down," I muttered. I pulled out my pockets. There was a receipt for gas. Nothing else.

"Ah well," I sighed. I started jotting down some notes.

David peered over my shoulder. "Have you thought about getting a notebook?"

NOTES FROM RUSSELL'S GAS RECIEPT

WHAT WE NEED TO KNOW ABOUT CUSTOMER SERVICE

There are three levels of service experience that companies can choose to create for their customers. The key word is "choose!" Choosing the top level, legendary service, builds the trust that gives you and your customers the opportunity to enjoy the full value of your relationship. Choosing less leaves your customer relationship wide open for your competition to walk in.

A commitment to legendary service experiences shapes your business. This commitment tells your entire organization that service is a role *and* a mindset that extends beyond your front line service staff and connects everyone in the company. When your team has a companywide, inside-out and outside-in understanding of that principle, they can deliver on your brand promise.

Customer service is an interpersonal experience. Service teams must apply a mix of situational thinking, skills, abilities, language, agility and technologies to their role. These roles are best developed within a customized service program, ensuring your brand promise is married to listening, responding and evolving with your customer's voice, thus building a depth of companywide capability, agility and speed to act.

WHAT CAN GO WRONG IN CUSTOMER SERVICE

You live in a fishbowl. Everything you and your service staff do is visible to the customer, from how you work together, to how healthy your water is.

If you choose to deliver less, you communicate that you devalue your customers and employees. Even worse, the "deliver less" paradigm will surface stories that stagnate the flow of performance throughout your fishbowl even more. By "stories" we mean mindsets and assumptions of the company and the company's "acceptable" level of service that are repeated and absorbed up and down your formal and informal communication channels and out into the world. When service stories that oppose your brand promise grow on the grapevine, your market position will be pulled deep into the weeds.

Your entire company is a service chain to the customer. From the CEO to the manufacturers to the front-line service staff, a company is ultimately about making customers happy, and enriching their lives. When any part of the service chain forgets the customer, your connection with the customer begins to fade.

When connections fade, conversations with the customer, and attitudes towards them, take on *a mindset, language* and *way of interacting* that is rehearsed and apathetic. When this happens, you'll start to hear a sound: the murmurs of a story, morphing into a feeding frenzy against your brand across word of mouth and social media, telling the story of how they left your company for your competitors.

While you're keeping your service chain connected to your customers, remember that your technology has to keep pace with customer service demands, and behaviour trends. To observe how important this is, look no further than the explosion of service apps in the market. Every day, these apps are an example of the speed of innovation in customer service technologies. They advance access and communications in any channel that the customer needs, and support the rapid development of transferring customer service details between multiple channels, giving customers access to start the conversation in one channel and complete it at their convenience in any channel and technology that suits their day. We may be a blink of the eye away from this being expectation in customer service, and misjudging the speed of this need will put your customer service experience trailing well behind the desired pace of your customer.

VALUE YOUR CUSTOMERS

Too often, companies adopt a mindset that service staff can keep pace with the evolution of customer needs with a narrow-brush training event. This approach is more aligned with status quo thinking than it is in valuing your customers. Status quo is dangerous. It's like stopping on the shoulder of a highway and letting everyone pass you by: a sure way to undermine a customer-centered business.

Instead, innovate. Do you engage in ongoing dialogue with customers about what they need to achieve in *their* business? Do you pull up a chair in meetings as a way for the customers' voice to contribute to important questions? Are you using this insight to value your customers and enhance service throughout the company *before your customers ask for it?* Develop your front-line staff to be legendary, and complement their new capability with a look at every segment of your customer value chain. Explore best practises from all angles, assumptions, and realities.

Whether it be your touchpoints, the customer's world, or your competitors, explore possibilities for a customer segmentation strategy that links customer growth and delivery of service to specific business and service analytics or other unique programs that fit your business. When you understand the big picture of customer behaviour and decisions along with your value contribution to their business, you have the insight to be *legendary*.

WHAT IS THE BIGGER PICTURE?

That's your choice!

In most organizations, we don't need to recreate the wheel. In your service chain, the "need" at every touchpoint is to aim towards legendary service. Align the customer's voice with the ongoing capture of insight that converts it into legendary service attitudes, behaviours and conversations. Building this capability is no different from legendary service itself; to masterfully execute what matters most, knowing what's needed and committing to doing it right, every time.

When actors deliver an award-winning, soul-searing, standing-ovation performance, it's not just them that deserve the applause: the men and women behind the scenes, working to fine-tune every element of the performance, have literally set the stage for the actors to succeed. When the audience leaves, telling all their friends how they loved the play, it's the behind-the-scenes folks that made it happen.

If you want to build legendary service, how you interconnect your behind-the-scenes coordination matters, too. Anticipating customer needs, creating insight, executing the right tasks in the right way: it all matters. Service development programs customized around the four key ingredients of legendary service will bring to life a significant resource of companywide customer knowledge, real-world situational service capability and agility to act. A customer-centered company who has built the capability to create legendary service will have also put in place the framework for perpetual accelerated learning through affirmation and coaching.

Within your fishbowl every interaction you have with customers builds the future of your brand. Your brand expands with the measurable value and images left in the mind of customers, and in the buzz from the stories they tell, whether it be through word-of-mouth, online reviews, or social media.

Make the legendary service experiences you provide the most challenging thing for a competitor to duplicate! Earn customer advocacy, and inspire raving fans!

BLIND SPOT FIVE
Building Teams Without Communication

On Thursday, I was humming a happy little tune to myself.

I'd had David in a couple more times to complete our customer service training, and the entire department was working nicely. He'd taught us how to seize what he called "learning moments" throughout the day, and shown me a few things to watch out for in the future. We still had some work to do to get the company where I wanted, but customer service was in great shape.

Close to five, I began to tidy up my office in preparation for leaving. I took my coffee mug to the kitchen to wash it out. On the way there, I came across the product development team.

"That's right," I said to myself. "They have a meeting today."

I decided to drop in.

The product development team met Thursdays and Fridays, when they were all free from their other duties. They usually met in the old board room, but since customer service had taken over it, now they used one of the unused sales rooms.

The product development team was fluid—but usually consisted of five core people: Rohit Binder in marketing, Gary Grant from finance, Jack O'Leary from manufacturing, and Dennis and Tina, the engineers.

I peeked in to the room, and saw these five sitting, standing, and lounging in different corners of the room. They were looking at a toaster.

I leaned against the doorframe. They were too engrossed in conversation to notice me.

"Can we add a Twitter feature?" That came from Rohit. The marketing director was looking at the wall, waving his hands at an ad campaign only he could see. "Maybe on an LCD screen? I have a perfect ad planned for that. And a retro fifties aesthetic! The hipsters would eat it up."

"The profit margin is a bit slimmer than what I'm comfortable with." Said Gary Grant. He sat on a swivel chair, legs crossed, leafing through a clipboard of figures.

"And these coils are too dense…" That was Jack O'Leary, the head manufacturing director. He stood over the toaster, arms crossed. He bit his lip. "We'll have to get a new alloy if we want to build it in our plant. And I don't know if we have the space for an extra ton of metal."

"The denser coils will halve the toaster's energy use." Countered Dennis Chu. He hovered over the toaster like a mother hawk. "And you've already taken out the insulation."

"I'd like to raise that issue again by the way," Tina interjected. "The insulation—"

This discussion seemed to be turning into an argument. I pushed off from the doorframe and entered the room.

"That's because you—"

"'Scuse me," I interjected.

"Well you said—"

"Hey." I cut in.

"—Blueberry muffins my foot!"

"Okay," I clapped my hands. "How's our new product line coming?"

The team turned to look at me. Suddenly, no one was talking.

And then everyone tried to talk at once.

"It's just—"

"These coils!"

"Can't possibly—"

I held up my hands. They kept talking.

"Muffins!"

"Coils!"

"Everyone wants Twitter!"

I slowly backed out of the room. The argument continued.

I strolled over to my office, and dialed a number.

It was no surprise the team was acting like this. They were, fundamentally, very different people. They had different professional experiences, different professional objectives, and different amounts of time and commitment to the project. Conflict was natural, maybe inevitable. But if we wanted to get that new product line out, I needed to get them on the same page.

"Hi, David?" I asked. "Will you be in the neighborhood tomorrow? You will? Well, think you have some time for impromptu training?"

The next day was Friday. David arrived at eight-thirty. The office was in a peaceful state: we didn't have any urgent business, and everyone was wrapping up their tasks neatly and quietly in preparation for the weekend.

I met David in the foyer and walked him over to where the team was once again hashing out a verbal wrangle.

"You said your product development team was having trouble?" David asked.

"That's right."

"And how've you been working with them so far?" David asked.

"Well—there was a job that needed to get done." I said. "So I just sort of brought them together. They're professionals. I admire their abilities, and I trust each of them individually. I figured they could sort it out organically."

David nodded. "It's great that you show that respect for your employees. But the organic approach can sometimes be an oversight if you're working with such a cross-functional team. Can you tell me more about them?"

I briefed David on each team member as we walked, and gave him a history of the team itself. I'd pulled it together about four months ago with the purpose of creating a line of our traditional products redesigned based on our customer feedback and our advances in energy efficiency; I felt it would really shake up the market in our favor. It should have been an easy task—but somehow, it had gone wrong.

We came to the team's room. The five were still arguing. I stood aside and waved David in.

"Okay everyone!" I smacked my palm on the door. The bang quieted them down.

"I am a concerned man right now." I said. "I know you. All of you. You're talented, and hardworking, and the best examples of our company talent. And you're arguing about muffins."

"So," I said. "It's time to become a team. This is David Boyce, and he's going to help us to do that."

The team members suddenly looked a bit embarrassed. I wondered if this was the power of bringing in an outside opinion.

As each team member settled down into a chair, David introduced himself and his professional experience before diving into the heart of the matter.

"Do you know why you're arguing?" David asked them. "From what Russell tells me, you all get along well on a personal level, and you're all talented and intelligent. So, why argue?"

No one answered. David leaned forward a bit. "No one?" He asked. "Do you mind if I share what it looked like a few minutes ago? You're not aligned around a common story. You're not aligned with 'why' you've been brought together. Without alignment, you're negating the opportunity to leverage the talent in this room to achieve that goal. Without alignment, you're not a team. Not yet."

I felt my own eyes widen a bit at that. David continued.

"There's a *big* difference between a team and a group of skilled, well-intentioned people." David said, walking across the room. "Right now, each of you is focused on your piece of the project. That's good. But, without a clear, unifying alignment to the big picture of why you've been bought together, this team will go like a bad football game. Think about it: if the linemen have one idea of the play, and the quarterback has a different idea, the thought of a touchdown is a painful pipedream."

David turned on his heel. "When I was with your customer service team, I learned how everyone here has a great story of what they do and how they create success."

David came to the centre of the room, and held out his hand. "But, right now you're telling yourselves *different stories of why you've been brought together*. When that happens, your real reason for being here will get lost in the different stories you're acting on."

David pointed out to Jack. "For example, you're acting on the story and team protocols of the manufacturing team who produces products efficiently and effectively."

David swung around to the engineers, Tina and Dennis. "And you two are acting on the story and team protocols of engineers who design new products that define your brand."

David held up his palms. "All of your stories of expertise and team protocols describe how you create functional value for the company. But do you know what? *They don't matter.* At least, they don't matter in this team. In this product development team, you will succeed when you operate with a story and protocols that align your thinking, unify your expertise, and aim squarely at your common purpose"–here David paraphrased my original direction to the team–"to lead the market in customer value, with a revolutionary product line that brings to life customer dreams and desires."

"This sounds a bit like the talk we had about customer service." I noticed.

David winked. "They're very neatly intertwined, actually, and I think our last talk has in many ways laid the groundwork for this one. I'm glad you kept my number in your phone contacts instead of writing it down on one of your scrap papers."

"Yes," I said to myself, musing. "Those scraps of paper are becoming like a curse for me. It's like they're some sort of running joke in the narrative of my life."

"Well, let's not go that far." David said. He addressed the team again. "For the rest of the day, I'd like to explore. We'll discover the story of what kind of team you want to be, and the protocols of team you need on this project.

"But we know why we're on this project." Gary interrupted. "We need to create a new product line."

"Yes." David said. "And why are you doing that? How does this project connect to the voice of the customer and reflect on the company brand? How would you describe this team's purpose? Or, what would you like it to be?"

David hit something there; the team was getting a bit more excited. They threw out a couple of ideas. This team was responsible for developing new products and improving existing lines. Their innovation kept the company competitive, and benefited the environment. That was their overwhelming purpose. As for what they thought the team could be? Well that was the cool part: they all wanted the same thing: a united purpose, an adaptable, agile team, and the ability to deliver and celebrate their results.

Then, David took them a bit deeper into that idea.

David asked what they believed in. Not in a moral or religious sense, but what they believed they could accomplish at Prism, and what they could do to deliver on what we knew of our customer's dreams and desires.

The answers almost made me tear up.

They believed the new home appliances can help families live the lifestyle of their dreams. They believed they could be beautiful, reliable, and counted on to help save the world. They believed they brought families together, strengthening the heartbeat of the home.

"And that," David said quietly. "Is the kind of thinking that makes brands famous. Now, let's talk about your customers. Who are they?"

"Retail chains that sell appliances." Dennis offered.

"And who are their customers?" David asked.

"Shoppers who want the best low-energy appliances." Tina answered.

"So!" David said. "This team's opportunity to advance the company's value is throughout your customer's organizations and their consumers' homes."

This generated a new discussion about value, and what the team could do to improve it. The conversation was reaching overflow when David held up his hand and asked a new question. "And what about your connection with other teams in your organization? How do we orient ourselves with them to create value?"

A new discussion began. This one focused on the culture and components of the company, and how the team could best fit the customer's voice and this project into it, benefiting our system as well as the customer.

David reigned in the discussion. "Okay, so now I'm getting a sense of what your story is. Once we have your story, we have your next task:

understanding your team roles—not just your functional roles, team roles—based on bringing that story to life."

He pointed to Gary. "What's your job?"

"Finance." Gary said. "I advise on financial matters."

"And your *role* is to make sure the customer gets the most value for their money." David explained. He turned to Dennis. "What's your job?"

"I design kitchen appliances." Dennis answered.

"And your *role* is to make sure the customer saves money on energy, and can rest assured that their kitchen appliances are helping the environment."

"See what I'm recommending?" David said. "Know your functional and team roles, and align all your ideas and actions around why you've been brought together—your purpose—and serve your roles and personal goals to keep the team moving toward success."

Now, David turned to me.

"Russell," David said. "I'd like to work with the team the rest of the day, and then connect with you at 4:45. I'd like to work with everyone to help them define who this team is, and the great work that's about to come."

"Thanks David. You do that." I shook his hand and turned to everyone. I said, firmly. "Everyone take notes on this to remember."

The team rustled in their bags and pockets. They all pulled out notebooks.

"Uh, and then could someone tear off a sheet for me." I said—slightly less firmly. Tina handed me a ruled page.

I went back to my office and made a few notes on Tina's paper. After that, I sat at my desk and reflected on what David said about unifying the team's purpose and story.

Then it hit me: these ideas didn't just advance our team's capability to act; they gave us the tools to create success for all our team initiatives. I thought about the service chain David had introduced me to earlier: how far up, and how far down could these initiatives create success? I got goose bumps thinking about the possibilities.

Ten minutes to five David knocked on my door. He looked animated, glowing with energy. I was struck again by the man's obvious passion for his work.

Athena Alliance Members

"David!" I said. "How'd it go?"

"It went well, they have a lot of passion for this project" David said, wiping his forehead. "And I just have one final process I'd like to share with you."

David took a seat opposite me.

"This team needs a champion." He said. "Not a leader per se, but someone who can gather them together. And I think you're in the ideal position for that."

"Well, I guess that's more or less in my job description," I said, grinning. "What would you like me to do?"

"I'm going to recommend a technique that can help you build team agility. There are few variations and I like to call my style 'Huddle-Ups.' It sets in place an innovative team mindset that connects the team to discover what's needed next." David said. He folded his hands on my table. "Do you watch a lot of sports?"

"Basketball." I said. I did a little fist-pump. "Let's go Raptors."

"Nice. Well, you know how a coach takes a timeout and brings the entire team together at critical moments in the game, to clarify their next play to win?" David asked. "What points to go for, how to get around the other team's system, what each team member needs to do next? That's what the team needs from you."

David elaborated. "Every morning, for fifteen minutes, lead Huddle-Ups with the team. Start with the team's purpose and ask each person to share what's going right and how it's being achieved. Next, each person can share their priority action that they will achieve by the end of the day. Then, surface team ideas for moving past any *minor* challenges that have been identified since the last huddle-up. Finally, affirm them, linking to how the team is living their story. From there, everyone is primed to achieve what's needed next by day's end. When a complex challenge surfaces, requiring contribution from other areas of the business, take them out of the Huddle-Ups and move them into an innovative session with the appropriate staff at another time that day. Do that every day for two weeks, and let me how it goes."

And so it went. Every day, I gathered the team. We connected to why we were a team and what we believed in. We built upon what went right to move us forward, and had clarity for what had to be completed next in each role. We affirmed our commitment to success. Our work was more focused, more efficient, and easier. And the machine that we called our business grew closer, and more organic, as the leaders on our project team transferred what David taught them into their functional teams. More than ever I felt we were a team, aligned with a common purpose, and story we believed in.

NOTES FROM RUSSELL'S (BORROWED) PAPER

NARRATIVES IN TEAMS

When David works with team leaders, someone will surface a common challenge: teams spend a good portion of their working hours tuned in to achieving their purpose, but they spend the rest exhausting energy—and relationships—trying to figure out how to work together or with others in the organization.

That's a lot of misplaced energy and time, and it happens because of differing narratives.

When teams first come together, each member brings different narratives with them. These narratives encompass their unspoken beliefs formed by past team experiences—good, bad and ugly. Narratives shape their assumptions of how they relate to the team, how the team relates to itself, and how the team relates to the business and its customers. When each team member acts on their own historical narrative, it can be as if the team's goals get swept up in the blast of a nor'easter; some make it through unscathed, most do not, and the best-laid plans get washed further out sea with the increasing intensity of each new wave.

Team leaders and team members need to plug in to a single narrative.

WORK *IN* AND *ON* TEAMS

Gallup recently indicated that as little as 11% of employees worldwide are engaged in their jobs. Eighty-nine percent float between "somewhat" to "fully" disengaged.

Low engagement reduces productivity, profitability, and customer and employee retention. Think of the damage that can do to a company's brand.

In this Gallup study, functional units and work teams who scored high in employee engagement had *double the opportunity for success* than those with low scores. Rather than disengaging staff around "what's wrong" or "who's wrong," leverage your team's story, purpose, protocols and goals to positively engage staff to work in and on the team. This dialogue affirms "what's right" so the team can leverage their strengths, explore customer needs, and align energy and action towards doing "what's needed next" to serve customers and each other.

WHAT A GOOD TEAM LOOKS LIKE

We can look at high performing teams like we look at the human body: a dynamic unit of function. A team's effectiveness and efficiency is the result of several interconnected components that, when aligned and encouraged, create ideal conditions for incredible cognitive, emotional and functional performance.

The best teams unite under a single narrative and *live it*, adding new chapters by the day. This narrative centers each member with agreement and passion for their purpose, their roles and connection to the voice of the customer. It maps how the team communicates within itself, and within the organization.

A team narrative thrives when team protocols are linked to why the team exists: their ultimate purpose. With all team members in attendance, the team collaborates to clearly define a set of team protocols. These protocols will define how the team will function with each other and with others to create success. These teams use their protocols as part of the *performance fabric*: they present and reference them during team meetings, huddle-ups, coaching, reviews and celebrations.

With protocols in place, the best teams align member goals and responsibilities with their ultimate purpose. Using their purpose and protocols as a guide, team members play a functional role *and* a team role committed to doing the right things and doing them right. When team members, or the team itself, gets off track, they openly hold each other up to the team's protocols as an opportunity to learn, improve, refocus and move forward.

The best teams develop as part of the daily flow of their life. Team learning means storytelling, diverse thinking, collaboration, feedforward, feedback, coaching, mentoring and candor are embraced as a valuable part of the team's dialogue. They map their network connections and leverage the organization's formal and informal communication channels, sharing expertise between teams at a minimum of one level up, a level down, and cross-functionally. They discover where their purpose, goals, and timelines align with others, create understanding of each other's protocols, and which players they are working with, and how to relate to them.

WHAT LEADERS CAN DO TO BUILD AND CONTINUALLY GROW TEAMS

To create a high-performing team, leaders must guide, or be an enthusiastic participant in, facilitated team discussions to set one narrative in place. And passionately share that story within the business and with customers. Supporting a customer-centric business, leaders benefit from engaging the team in exploration to define who the customers are and why they buy from you, who their customer's serve, and how their team purpose and accomplishments contribute to the enrichment of the customer's lives.

Leaders are also the stewards of change. Countries, industries, companies, customers, and competitors live in a never-ending state of flux. Teams need to live there as well—advancing capability and agility within the four stages of teaming. Leaders of high-performing teams guide team evolution through these stages with a conductor's precision. With a wave, a pass, and a careful hand, they manage the growth and evolution of the people and process—dimming, tensing, and building to a crescendo through all the stages of team growth.

No matter the location along the customer chain, leaders deepen team insight by understanding and connecting to the customer voice; during meetings, bring two empty chairs to the table. One chair represents the customer's voice. The second chair the other teams in your company. Include them to surface a 360-degree perspective of your thinking, questions, solutions and actions. Better still, invite them to join the meeting now and then.

A final item that leaders can accomplish is to set the bar high for teams! Drew Houston CEO of Dropbox has said "You become the average of the 5 people you hang out with." Be sure to set your 'teaming' bar high so your team's average is no less than awesome!

TEAMS CHANGE—EVEN WHEN MEMBERS STAY THE SAME

Teams can diligently set their protocols, roles and goals, understand their piece of the company's strategy and then move ahead. When they do this, they assume that the team is "set" for the year. How far back in your thinking do you need to go to recall when we lived in that reality?

External conditions can change a team throughout their work together: so much so that the team you end a project with might be completely different from the one you started with—even if the team hasn't changed its members!

For example, conditions that will create a need for you to be a different team include: a new budget, a new customer to support or loss of an important customer, a misunderstanding of team protocols, when the air in the room during meetings feels heavy and stale. Other conditions include when team members are unaware of how to contribute in their functional and team roles, when cross-functional teams change staff, purpose or protocols, or when the stories within your team or with cross-functional teams are beginning to take a back seat to stories on the company's grapevine.

In the same vein, conditions that will create the need for you to be an entirely new team include: a change in team purpose, a change in team members, and a change in the company's strategic direction or a sudden shift in competitive landscape.

The team you are today will not be the team your company and customers will need you to be tomorrow, next month, next quarter, or next year. Be it your purpose for being, roles, responsibilities, results, members or other teams you work with, a need to develop into a different or new team is coming your way. Leaders and team members who make it a way of life to work *IN* and *ON* their team will have the capability and agility within to anticipate and respond a new when the game changes.

BLIND SPOT SIX
Ignoring Health and Safety at the Office

"So, you think you've gotten a handle on these "U-turns," as you call them?" Cindy asked.

I put down my chopsticks and thought about it.

Cindy and I both happened to be visiting downtown today: she was going to a seminar, and I was meeting with some clients later. I'd wanted to thank her for her help, so I'd offered to buy her lunch at Rol San restaurant: the best dim sum place in the city.

Over steaming shrimp dumplings and simmering chicken feet, I told her the story of how I'd come up with the term "U-turns." They were knowledge gaps—old preconceptions that executives needed to reverse—or "make a U-turn"—to get back on track and coast smoothly through their careers. Thanks to Cindy and the other members of the Athena Alliance, I'd made every U-turn I'd ever need. From networking, to personal branding, to customer service and beyond, I could confidently say that I'd learned everything I needed to.

"Yep," I leaned back. "I think I have everything under—hurk!"

"Russell?" Cindy asked.

I couldn't breathe.

I stood up, suddenly dizzy. The restaurant swam in front of my eyes. The details of my plate—half finished dumplings and drops of soy sauce—swirled in my vision. I felt a thump-thump-thump on my temples.

"Oh my goodness you're choking. Here." Cindy came up behind me. Her hands wrapped around my stomach.

Cindy squeezed. I coughed. Suddenly, I could breathe again.

"That was amazing." I said. I rubbed my throat. There was lingering, fuzzy pain there. "Thank you!"

"Oh, it's nothing." Cindy said. She patted my on the back. "You okay?"

"Yes." I coughed. "My goodness, where'd you learn that?"

"One of our trainers is a health and safety expert." Cindy said. "I went to one of his first-aid courses. There's also a way to do the Heimlich maneuver yourself if you're alone. Let me show—"

"I'm good," I said, putting up my hands. I coughed a bit more, and sat back down. "Wow. Thank you again."

We finished up our lunch and went our separate ways. As I walked out, two things occurred to me. One: maybe I needed a better term than "U-turn". Two: I didn't know everything just yet.

A week later, I confirmed my suspicion.

I was eating a Big Mac at my desk, just zoning out and watching my screensaver bounce a flying toaster around, when I had a thought.

If I choked on this Big Mac right now, who would save me?

Nancy strolled by the door.

"Nancy," I called her over. "Do you know first aid?"

"Nope," Nancy said. "But we have four people in the office who do. It's the law actually"

"But I've never heard of that law." I said, putting down my burger. "In fact, aside from those first-aid folks, I bet no one knows where our kits are, or what to do in case of an emergency."

We thought about this for a moment. As we did, we heard a siren.

I got up and peered out the window. A fire engine roared down the road.

"Nancy," I said, carefully. "Where's our fire extinguisher?"

"… I don't know." Nancy admitted.

I finished my lunch and made a call.

"Cindy?" I said. "It's Russell again. You mentioned that one of your trainers taught you first aid? Can they train other safety topics as well? Super. Could you put me in touch with him for an appointment tomorrow?"

Dean Turner arrived the next day at noon.

I met Dean in the foyer. Cindy had told me a bit about him: originally a first aid instructor with the Department of National Defense, he'd spent 22 years in the army, training soldiers for twelve years before seeking out even more knowledge and forming his own company. Now, this company was an approved first aid and health and safety provider, provincially and federally.

"You must be Russell!" Dean said. We shook hands. "Cindy told me all about you. Now, what can I do for you?"

"Well… I just became aware of how important health and safety is in the workplace." I said. "Acutely aware. I want to make sure we're safe at our office, and in our plant. After all, these people are my responsibility."

"That's very responsible sentiment." Dean said. "But I think that through working with me, you'll find that safety is everyone's responsibility. Everyone from you, to the average worker, to the designated first aid responder."

He stuck his thumbs in his pockets and gave a quick glance around. "Now, to give you an introduction of my company: we specialize in three areas of health and safety: policy programs, training, and products."

"Why don't you tell me a bit about training?" I suggested. I lead Dean into the main office. A few heads popped out of the cubicles as we passed by. I gave a little wave to everyone.

I took Dean to the main thoroughfare between the kitchen, the cubicles, and the offices. From here, we could see into everything. I noticed Dean take appraising glances at certain places: the carpets, the cabinets, the windows, common places where people could trip and fall.

Dean nodded. "To start with, we can train you and your staff to safely handle emergencies, and to control your equipment and environment to prevent emergencies from happening."

"You mean first aid." I said.

"Exactly." Dean said. "But there's even more to safety than just handling an emergency. We also have courses in WHMIS, fire extinguisher training, and fall arrest. This training ensures that accidents don't happen at all. We also train in marine safety, but I don't think you'll need that."

"The aquatic division of the company never panned out." I joked. "So, if I wanted to enroll our staff in one of those programs, what would it cover?"

"In our training programs, we cover the theoretical knowledge and practical skills." Dean said. He held out his hands. "Both are important. For example, in fall arrest training, we'll get you acquainted with the related legislature in OSHA—that's the Occupational Health and Safety Act—and we'll teach you how to actually not hurt yourself in the situation. The action part is especially important for us. It's important that when an accident happens, there's an internal responsibility system. A person won't be frozen with shock from an accident—instead, they'll have the mental capacity to act. That's what our training is for."

I nodded. It occurred to me that there was a lot of legislature that I didn't know about regarding health and safety. It wouldn't be enough to just have Dean come in once, I decided. I'd have to have Nancy organize some sort of regular check-up system.

"That's good." I said. "Training like that would be especially useful at our plant."

Dean grinned. "If you like, I can meet again with your head of manufacturing as well, and have this conversation with him, too."

"I'd like that." I said. "For now, let's focus on the office."

We stepped into the kitchen. Dean did a scan of the room, and I made one myself: no electrical wires exposed, no looming boxes ready to fall on people, no chipped tiles waiting to trip people up. I began to feel pretty confident about safety at Prism's office.

"Inside your office, we can make sure you have an appropriate number of people are trained in first aid." Dean continued. "We also do recertification training for first aid."

"And what about supplying the actual equipment?" I asked. "I mean, the bandages and such?"

I gestured to the far wall of the kitchen, to our first-aid kit. Our kit was a white box screwed into the wall. Dean deftly unlatched it and swung the top open. He probed through the contents, counting bandages and fingering packs of spacey-looking equipment.

"There are a few things missing here," he murmured. He checked a tag at the back. "Last updated... 2001."

I clenched my jaw. 2001 was when I joined the company. Suddenly, I wasn't so confident about Prism's safety features.

"That's not good, I imagine." I said.

"It is highly important to keep your kit up-to-date." Dean said. "Tell you what, we can come in and install one, and give it a check-up every sixty to ninety days. We can also inspect your plant, and make sure you have the proper stuff there. You know—eye wash stations, burn kits, stuff like that."

"We can't just put a standard first aid kit at the plant?" I asked.

"I'd recommend you have a kit tailored for industrial environments." Dean said. He shrugged. "Different incidences, you know?"

"One more thing." Dean said. He carefully latched the first aid kit shut. "There is something my company is trying to pioneer—defibrillators. You have to keep them properly serviced, and have people equipped with the training to use them, but in an emergency, they can make a crucial difference in saving someone from a heart attack."

I thought about the Big Mac on my desk. It was the third I'd eaten this week.

"Fair enough..." I murmured.

Dean toured around the office with me some more. We looked at high-risk areas for falls and slips, and we discussed how to organize the office a bit better to remove obstacles and potential hazards in an emergency. We ended the tour in my office.

Dean beamed. He gave a quick look around and swept his hands across the room. "And this," he said. "Is the most important place for health and safety to take place: planning and policy from the top."

"Good policy cuts off emergencies before they happen, right?" I asked.

"Yes." Dean said. "It also makes sure you're in line with provincial law if you get audited. There's a whole lot of policy that people can forget about in their day-to-day lives. And it's all spread across different pieces of legislature."

"Alright, alright." I said. I offered Dean a seat. "I ignored this one, because it seems like the most work. But it sounds like I should just tackle it: what do I need to know about policy?"

"It's a huge topic." Dean said. "But to be brief: health and safety is a requirement by the law. That's a good thing, by the way. Before these mandates came about, a lot of workers were getting injured."

"Good news we have these regulations then," I said. I sat down at my own desk and brushed aside my lunch. "But, I have to say, I'm a bit fuzzy on the specifics of it."

Dean nodded. "Most people know that it's important, but just never get around to diagnosing their policies, because of all the complexity."

"So, what's your diagnosis of us?" I asked.

"I think you're just a regular company." Dean said. He shrugged. "You know health and safety is important, but you're not always sure of how to implement it. With our help, we can cover everything from policy, to training, to equipment. We have a tool on our site I can introduce you too, if you like, and I can implement any measures you'd like to take."

I nodded. "I think we're going to need a lot of help here. I'd like you to coach us on policy—over here and at the plant, just to be sure—and then we'll move on to coaching more people how to respond quickly if something comes up. I want us all to know about this."

I had a sudden thought. "I should write this down."

I looked around but the only paper I could find was a Big Mac wrapper (I'd been busy that week—McDonald's was my go-to source of food). I found a pen, and started scribbling on it.

NOTES FROM RUSSELL'S BIG MAC WRAPPER

WHY SAFETY IS IMPORTANT

Just because you can't see the potential hazards in your office doesn't mean they don't exist. Take a closer look. That exposed wire could start a fire. That poor posture could slowly damage nerves and cartilage.

An accident on the job can put people out of work. Severe injuries can impair them for life. Your talent is your most valuable resource, and it's your duty to make sure they work in a safe environment.

It's also the law. Across Canada, different federal and provincial ministries all audit companies for safe working conditions. And that's a good thing: before these mandates, many younger workers suffered injuries on the job. Now, accidents have decreased significantly across Canada and the US. Still, heavy fines exist for workplaces that can't meet health and safety requirements. Larger companies can implement these requirements easily, but smaller and medium-sized companies can have problems in this field.

AREAS TO FOCUS ON

Policy: good policy can prevent accidents from happening in the first place. Review your health and safety guidelines with a qualified professional to assess that you're doing your best to keep your employees safe. Also remember that there's usually specific legislature for dealing with specific equipment. While large businesses can devote significant resources to developing policies internally, small and medium-sized businesses can have trouble wading through all the information. Call an expert to see if you can benefit from policy training.

Training: under provincial law, it's mandatory to have a certain number of people equipped with knowledge of first aid. But legality aside, it's just safer to have people who know what to do in an emergency. First aid training covers topics that include shock, choking, and heart attack.

Equipment: even if you study how to use a defibrillator, that training won't help you unless you have one. Also, unless that defibrillator is maintained, it won't do the job it was designed for. Keep your health and safety equipment up to date around the office, and customize your equipment for different working environments.

COMMON SAFETY TIPS

Prevent falls. Loose carpeting, stray power cords, stairs without adequate guardrails, spills, tight spaces, and wandering chairs. These tiny things are hard to spot until you trip over them. Scan your office for potential tripping hazards.

Prevent ergonomic strain. Carpal Tunnel Syndrome isn't fun. Neither is back, neck, or eye strain. Give employees time to stretch, and give them ergonomic equipment to prevent strain.

Meet First Aid requirements. In most cases, a business must have a certain percentage of staff who know first aid. Make sure you have your people trained, and make sure your first aid equipment is well stocked and up to date. Check your provincial safety requirements for specific regulations.

BLIND SPOT SEVEN
Writing Without a Purpose

"New report, Russell," Nancy said, knocking at my open door.

I looked up from the report I was reading. "Oh. Thanks, Nancy."

"Ugh." I pulled the red pen out of my mouth. " Sorry about that. Thank you, Nancy."

Nancy handed me a sheaf of papers. They felt warm from the printer. I lay them down on the pile.

Nancy circled around and peered over my shoulder. "Lots of red marks." She commented.

"Yep." I put down my pen, took off my reading glasses, and sighed. The report slipped out of my hand, page by page.

My desk was engulfed in paper—paper littered with grammatical errors—that I'd highlighted with my trusty red pen.

In two weeks, I was scheduled to deliver a presentation to some visiting investors from America. The presentation would cover our plans for expansion, detail our advances in R&D, and—I hoped—convince them that investing more capital in Prism was the smartest, safest way to spend their money.

To that end, I'd asked the department heads to write a series of reports. These reports would be handed out to the investors at the meeting. Each report would detail a unique aspect of Prism's past success, and future aspirations.

The problem was, none of my heads knew how to write a sentence. I'd spent the last two hours trying to fix all the tiny errors in their writing, and mistakes were still coming in.

"You don't look too happy." Nancy said, leaning on my desk.

"I'm not feeling very happy." I sighed, and rubbed my temples. "Look: this sentence runs on for two paragraphs. I still don't know how they managed that. And I still don't know what it's supposed to mean."

"Bad writing is endemic to most people working in business," Nancy commented.

"But why?" I asked. "I don't have these problems."

"Well, you're a special case." Nancy observed. "And you read the newspaper a lot. That might help."

"You know," I picked up my red pen and wagged it at Nancy. "I spend a lot of time trying to figure out what our people are saying in their emails and reports. That must add up to a lot of wasted time. Think about it: if I spend ten minutes a day working out their meaning, then that's fifty minutes a week. There are four weeks in a month, so… multiply that by twelve months a year…"

I counted with my fingers and groaned. "I waste two hundred hours every year trying to figure out bad writing."

Nancy patted my shoulder. "Hang in there, boss. I'll clear some time and try to help out later."

I held up my hand. "We're not going to do that." I said. "I'm the CEO of this company. And you're the head of HR. We have more important things to do than proofread."

Nancy raised her eyebrows. "Going to call someone?"

"I think I might." I said. I whipped out my cell and keyed in Cindy's number.

"Hi Cindy?" I asked. "I need some help training my senior team…"

The next day, Geoff Weinsten was sitting across my desk.

Geoff was an expert in business communication. Yesterday on the phone, Cindy had promised me he'd solve problems I didn't even know I had. We had twelve days until the investors came, so I immediately signed Geoff on for a two-day session with my senior team. Today was our first day.

When I met Geoff this morning, he struck me instantly as easy-going and friendly. We were both family men, and talked about our kids on the way up the elevator. I was also a bit envious of his perfectly-formed goatee.

To prep for the workshop, I'd shown Geoff the error-filled reports. As he looked over them, I outlined the grammatical bootcamp I'd envisioned for my staff.

"Give them everything: ambiguous pronouns, dangling participles—even the dashes." I said. "After you're done with them, I want them to name modal verb forms in their sleep."

"Grammar is an important part of good communication." Geoff said. He leafed through the pages, and nodded to himself. "But I think your communication problems go deeper."

"But look," I said, pointing out a clump of red marks on the page in his hand. "See those comma splices? That random list of bullet points?"

"Yep. And it's important that we solve these issues." Geoff agreed. "And my training sessions cover good grammar. But you've got it back to front. Mastering the mechanical elements won't get to the root of bad communication, and it won't necessarily make your team's writing better after I leave."

"How do you mean?" I asked.

Geoff put down the pages. "Here's how I understand it: you want your team to write clearly, informatively, and persuasively. You want them to use their writing to influence action, not just fill up space on a page."

"That sums it up pretty well." I conceded.

Geoff continued. "But writing like that requires more than correct communication: it requires *influential communication*. When you can tap into that, you can do some amazing things."

"Hmmm." I looked over the mounds of paper still on my desk. "Move mountains, maybe?"

Geoff smiled. He put his hands on my desk and pushed himself up. "Maybe. I have to go set up the projector in the boardroom. I'll see you in an hour."

An hour later, I was seated at the side of our boardroom. My senior team was scattered around the conference table: Rohit Binder from marketing, Dennis Chu the engineer, Gary Grant from finance, and Austin Schwartz—another financial guy. I was a bit leery of their body language. They were slouched all over the place. Some were checking their emails.

I didn't have long to worry. Geoff came in thirty seconds later. He pulled the door shut behind him, introduced himself, and turned on his projector. Three words flashed on our screen.

Trust.

Logic.

Passion.

"Trust. Logic. Passion." Geoff said. "With those elements, you can move mountains. But why stop there? With those elements, you can influence the mountains to move themselves."

Geoff paused to let it sink in.

"Have any of you read Aristotle?" He asked, pressing his palms together.

They shook their heads.

"Well," Geoff pressed on. "Aristotle nailed the three elements of influential communication before the English language even existed. He called those elements ethos, logos, and pathos. But for our purposes, we'll call them trust, logic, and passion."

Geoff clicked to the next slide. It displayed a circle with TRUST, LOGIC, and PASSION circling around it. "And here's the kicker: if you're missing one of these three elements in your writing, you're not going to get people to act on your words."

Geoff counted down the three on his fingers. "It starts with trust. Without trust, you don't have a relationship, and without a relationship, you're no more influential than that telemarketer who calls during dinner. Only after you establish trust can you convince people to listen."

"After trust comes logic." Geoff continued. "Logic is the nuts and bolts of your message. Your readers expect you to deliver rock-solid logic so their brains can analyze what you're saying. Finally, you need to ignite your logic with a healthy dose of passion—your convictions and beliefs. The passion is the fuel that creates a sense of urgency and inspires your reader to get up and start moving."

I leaned forward. It was a fascinating model. But I was worried that my team still hadn't bought in to the idea. But that's when Geoff turned things around.

Geoff held up a finger. "Look at what I have here."

Geoff bent down, reached beneath the projector, and pulled out a cardboard box. Loose paper brimmed out the top.

Geoff clunked the box down on the desk. The wood shook a bit. A few scraps of paper drifted from the top and glided around the room.

"These are your reports!" He said. "Memos! Emails! All of them lacking in one or more of the three elements. These represent a month of communication at this office, but I bet the writing was so poor you can't remember a word from any of them—even though it was you who wrote them."

"Think of all the clutter. Think of all the overloaded details here. But," Geoff continued. "Why do we write like this when it plainly doesn't work?"

Someone raised their hand—Austin Schwartz.

"We've always written like this." Austin said. "They never taught us Aristotle in high school English. And when I studied commerce they just wanted my essay to have two thousand words."

Geoff nodded. "That's exactly the problem."

"You've been lied to." Geoff said. "All your lives, you've been told that good communication is formal, academic, and dry. You've been told to squeeze as many details as possible onto a page, and to use words that prove you have an advanced vocabulary."

"But really, that doesn't work." Geoff pointed to the pile of papers as proof. "Fundamentally, communication isn't about impressing people with your fancy words. It's not about cramming as much information as possible into a page. It's not even about reaching a self-imposed word count. It's about influence."

"And how do we influence people?" Geoff held up his palms. "Trust. Logic. Passion."

Rohit raised his hand again. "So, can we break that down into paragraphs? Like—one out every three paragraphs. One is logic, one is passion—"

"Well, it's not that clean." Geoff said. "It is true that every message requires those three elements. But, in each message, you'll use a different blend—a different amount—of each, depending on your situation."

"For instance." Geoff turned to me. "If you're a leader with a new strategy, and you need your team to follow you to the ends of the Earth, you'll need to use more passion to get them as excited as you are."

"And if you're communicating with a new client," Geoff turned around to face Austin. "You'll need to spend more time establishing trust and credibility; a client is more likely to be influenced by someone they trust."

"Finally," Geoff turned to Dennis. "If you're talking to your technical folks during a project meeting, you'll emphasize logic, because that's how technical folks think."

"All of these scenarios require all three elements at play." Geoff concluded. "You can't forgo trust, logic, or passion in anything you say. It's just a question of how much. In the reports I just looked at though, I saw too much focus on logic, at the expense of the other elements. What I recommend is a new, more balanced approach."

"And this approach will get people to do what we want." Rohit murmured.

"Except, they'll actually be doing what *they* want." Geoff corrected him. "That's the beauty of real influence."

Geoff turned back to the box. "You influence people, ultimately, when you make your message all about them. But every report in that box has too much logic, way too much content, way too much verbiage; and very few of those reports have done anything to establish a relationship, or to create any kind of urgency. It's all just a bunch of information."

"But it can be *easier*." Geoff pressed on. "So much easier. You can use these elements to light a fire." Geoff tapped his chest. "In here. And when you mix those elements, your people will come along with you willingly—without a fight."

"So, are you all feeling influenced right about now?" Geoff asked.

I looked around the room. My team wasn't slouching anymore. They weren't checking their email; they were listening to Geoff's every word.

"You know..." I said. "I think we are."

"Excellent," Geoff said. He twined his fingers and stretched them out. "Then, we'll get a bit more granular from here. I'm going to show you how to take these three elements and organize your thoughts into a logical structure. We're going to talk about how to write clear, concise sentences. And, of course, we're going to cover grammar and punctuation, but only in the context of how they help you be more influential. I promise you: I'm not going to force you to re-learn a bunch of rules they taught you in grade school.

Geoff began to break down the mechanics of persuasion. The concrete elements that created abstract forces like charisma and passion. He talked about the difference between a helpful detail and a needless one. And as he did, I surreptitiously nabbed a scrap of paper from the box, and scribbled notes.

NOTES FROM RUSSELL'S SCRAP PAPER

WHAT IS GOOD BUSINESS COMMUNICATION?

Good communication isn't about using the newest buzzwords, squeezing words onto a page, or even using semicolons properly. Instead, good business communication seeks to influence others, whether it be taking a particular action in corporate strategy, or just reminding people to clean out the fridge.

THE THREE ELEMENTS OF INFLUENTIAL COMMUNICATION

Aristotle named three qualities of rhetoric: ethos, logos and pathos. In English, we can reconfigure that to mean trust, logic, and passion.

Trust gives you the power to be heard. People will only listen to someone who they trust, professionally, and personally. After you gain people's trust, sound logic shows them that your argument makes sense. Finally, passion, and the ability to ignite it in others, will get listeners to accept your ideas, and act on them.

THE THREE HABITS WE NEED TO BREAK

If we want to become the best communicators we can be, we have to break three old habits.

Be concise, not verbose: a good report isn't necessarily a long report. 2000 word essays have conditioned us to think that way. In reality, a good message says everything it has to, in as few words as possible.

Use clear words, not fancy ones: fancy words won't win points: no one can understand them, and you don't look more professional for using them. Instead, opt for plain, clear English.

Include relevant details, not every detail under the sun: irrelevant details should stay out of your writing. *Relevant* details matter a lot. But overloading your reader with every bit of information you can think of will just waste everyone's time.

BLIND SPOT EIGHT
Talking Without Listening

"Russell?" Nancy called. "Do you have a minute?"

I stood in the centre of our cubicle farm. Around me, our office buzzed like a beehive. When Nancy had called out to me, I was holding three conversations at once with representatives from customer service, finance, and marketing.

Nancy waved at me from the end of the office. I waved back at her.

"Can't talk now Nancy," I said. "Sorry! Can it wait until lunch?"

"Well, I tried to bring it up yesterday," Nancy said, coming forward through the mess of people. "And I think it's urgent."

"Do you?" I said. "Dennis? Can you get me that—oh, you have it? Good, let me see."

Dennis passed along a progress report for our new product line. They were ready to start making prototypes.

"Good." I said. I passed the report back to him. "Send me an email tonight about time, including when we can meet again to run some tests." Dennis nodded and jogged away.

Nancy pushed through the crowd, shouldered past Dennis and ended up next to me.

"You know, Russell." Nancy said over my shoulder. "With all of these new hires, I think it's getting harder for us to communicate."

"You don't say," I murmured, inspecting a few printouts Rohit just handed me. I took out my pen and made a few squiggles on it. "But life's funny, eh?"

"And it's not just my opinion." Nancy continued. She stood up on her tip toes as I turned my back to her. "Since we boosted our customer

Athena Alliance Members

service staff, we've been getting more favorable reports from the clients, but the staff are starting to feel alienated from their managers."

"Indeed." I said, turning back.

"And I think that if this continues, they're not going to be as motivated." Nancy said. "And that will undo all of the training we did earlier to make them amazing in the first place."

"Nancy, you're an expert in your field." I said. Austin Schwartz handed me another document. "You do whatever you feel is necessary."

"Well… Can I borrow your pen?" Nancy asked, pointing to Athena Alliance pen I stuck in my shirt pocket.

"Oh," I said. "Sure thing. But I'll need it back later—I want to call Cindy about training for sales. I want to increase our sales staff in a few months."

"I'll bring it back." Nancy assured me.

"Okay," I said to Austin, "now, what's this about again?"

The office was bustling.

It had been like this for weeks. Since we upped our customer service staff and our salespeople, the phones had been ringing and our staff had been talking nonstop. Standing in the customer service hub, it was hard to even think with all the chatter going on.

It was beautiful.

All my professional life, I'd worked in quiet offices, sleepy cubicles, and dull boardrooms. I wanted to get as far away from quiet as possible.

There were *some* downsides of course. For some reason, I was doing a lot more talking, but not getting as much results. And for another, I was spending a lot more time sending and receiving emails. A lot more; I'd even bought another Blackberry—to handle file downloads on one, and do calls with the other. But, if that was the price of a noisy office, then I was glad to pay it; noise meant progress.

Two weeks later, Nancy knocked on my office door.

"Russell." Nancy said, leaning in. "I'm sending out Anita to get some snacks for the training seminar. Do you want anything?"

"A training seminar?" I asked.

"That's right. For you and some other senior staffers. As the head of my department and an expert in my field, I felt it necessary. I also arranged a personal consultation with you."

"This is news." I said, folding my hands over my desk. "When did we agree on this?"

"Don't you remember, Russell?" Nancy asked innocently. "I mentioned it three times last week."

I dimly recalled Nancy saying something about that. And maybe signing off on the event in an email.

"Ah. Well, I guess I'll be there?" I asked.

Nancy smiled. "Actually, I arranged for the trainer to meet you personally before the presentation. She's from Athena Alliance. Her name is Carrol Suzuki."

Nancy stood aside. Carrol Suzuki walked into the office. She was a mature woman, dressed chic in a red blazer over a black turtleneck.

"Hello there," Carrol said. She held out her hand. "Russell Baxter? Cindy's told me about you."

"I'll leave you two to talk." Nancy said. She backtracked out of the room as I invited Carrol to sit down.

"Um, yes." I said. Carrol settled into the chair opposite me. "Now, I've been pretty busy lately. Could you remind me what today's seminar is going to be about?"

"Listening." Carrol said simply.

There was something about how Carrol spoke, I noticed. She kept her volume low, but her words had depth in their intonation. I felt she could whisper in a busy subway station, and I'd still hear her voice.

"Listening?" I asked. "That is important!"

"I'm glad you think so." Carrol said.

I leaned back in my chair and rested my head on my palms. "I've often thought that if more people listened to me, this world would be a better place." I mused.

"Actually." Carrol said, smiling. "The purpose of this seminar was to teach the senior staff to listen more to their teams."

"Oh." I deflated a little. "Well, that's good too, I guess."

"You say a lot by how you listen." Carrol said. She leaned forward, and laid her palms flat on one knee. "People usually think listening is a passive activity. They feel that it's talking that solves problems. But, that's not true. When you listen, you're actually communicating lots of things."

"What sort of things do we communicate?" I asked.

"For instance…" Carrol said. "Right now, your listening pattern suggests you're not too interested in talking to me. You're bouncing your leg up and down. And you glance at your clock every ten seconds. To top it off, the mode you state your questions with is pretty close-ended. You're here, but you don't seem very engaged in the conversation."

I straightened up. I noticed that my leg was indeed bouncing.

"Sorry." I said, and meant it.

"No, no, it's no problem." Carol said.

"I didn't mean—I came across as rude just now. I'm sorry." I said. "It's just that it's been so busy lately. And anyway—wait a minute, I remember now. Nancy was worried about this. Am I acting like this to all of my team?"

Carrol didn't confirm or deny anything. She didn't need to.

"Okay," I breathed. "Listening. Maybe the way we listen does say a lot. So I have to learn how to be more still when other people are talking?"

"Not quite." Carrol said. "Intentional listening, the kind I believe in, is all about aligning three things: what do I intend? What do I show? And what do I say as an intentional listener?"

Carrol picked up her bag and stood up. "Why don't we walk to the boardroom?"

I followed Carrol out of my office. Before I left, I gave a longing glance at my two Blackberries: they were on desk, all alone. My babies. I reached over to pick them up, then stopped myself.

"No," I muttered to myself. "I'm going to concentrate on this."

Carrol seemed to know the layout of the office. She took me by the HR hub. Nancy was talking to a new representative.

"Look at Nancy." Carrol said. "Notice how she responds to the other person's words with nods and encouragement? Oh—look, see how she just asked that follow-up question and clarified her own understanding? You can see that she's interested, and she's going to get more and better results from her staff. And I bet she's also asking the right sort of questions to clarify her understanding."

"Right," I murmured. "But, this seems like pretty subconscious behavior. Can we actually train people to become more engaged listeners?"

"I think by changing outer habits, the inside changes as well. Then it becomes second nature." Carrol said. She continued walking.

"When I see my granddaughter," Carrol said. "Her parents make a point that she stops her video games to come and talk to me. At that time, my granddaughter might be thinking "I'd rather play my videogames" but one day, she'll internalize those external behaviors, and the meaning behind them."

"You know, my parents were the same way," I mused. "And after a while, it just became natural for me to pay attention to my grandparents."

"Exactly." Carrol said. "The inside catches up."

We walked by the finance cubicles. Austin and Dennis were talking about the new product line. This conversation didn't look so good; each of them was shutting down the other, frantically trying to get their own thoughts out instead of building a conversation. Was this why our release for the new prototypes had gone off schedule?

"You mentioned good questions." I said. "What sort of questions are 'good' ones?"

"I'll go over it more in the seminar today," Carrol said. "But I don't like to call something a 'bad question.' When you ask a question, it's still good that you're even asking! That being said: there are questions that are more effective than others. These questions bring out someone's knowledge and perspective to get good ideas out of them, instead of trying to put your ideas in their heads. When you draw people's ideas out, they become more engaged. And when they're more engaged, you influence the buy-in you get from others when we discuss an idea."

"That's powerful stuff coming from something as simple as conversation." I said.

We came back to my office.

"Conversation is a powerful tool," Carrol said. "It's what allows us to share ideas and collaborate to produce great things. But without listening, we're not really having a conversation, or building a consensus."

"I understand," I said. I leaned against my desk. "So, how do I start transforming my listening then?"

"You already took the first step by realizing there was an issue to address." Carrol said. "Now, we'll go over some exercises and activities to train intentional listening habits. After some follow-up sessions, you'll start to notice a definite change."

"The inside catches up." I murmured. "Alright then."

I idly picked up one of my Blackberries. As I did, it vibrated in my hand.

"Oh," I clicked my phone. "I have an email. It's from Nancy. And it says… Everyone should be at the board room in five minutes."

I chuckled, and slipped the phone into my pocket. "Carrol, if you're ready to start, I'd love to introduce you to everyone."

The session went well. Carrol spoke about the importance of listening, how to identify problems, and exercises for building our intentional listening skills. After the session, I jotted some notes down on the whiteboard.

Those notes stayed up the next day, and the day after that. And as we passed the whiteboard day after day, I began to notice a change in my team.

I noticed a lot more pausing. I noticed a lot more clarification. I also noticed that I was talking a lot less, but a lot more was getting done.

Two weeks later, I copied the notes from the whiteboard for my own files, and erased the words off the board. After that, I expected the team to forget about the lessons we'd learned, but they stuck with them. Carrol was right: the inside catches up.

NOTES FROM THE WHITEBOARD

WHY WE NEED TO LISTEN

Listening is about uncovering assumptions that people have that will get in the way of them buying in to a decision. It uncovers barriers or obstacles that we hadn't thought about before. It identifies better ideas than any one person can have. In fact, by taking the time to listen, we can go faster towards a goal than we would otherwise.

Listening is not merely a passive activity. It's just your quiet contribution to a conversation. And when we forget to make that contribution, we can lose respect, lose valuable information, and otherwise lose business. On the other hand, if we can listen with intent, we are more likely to create the kinds of impacts we truly need to be effective and successful. For leaders, intentional listening leads to better results, greater respect, and stronger relationships. In the long term, listening plays a large part of making a leader effective.

HOW DO WE CHECK OURSELVES?

We often fall into patterns for listening. The tricky part about patterns is that you don't know you're in one—or if that pattern is keeping you from making an impact and getting results from other people.

Record yourself in a candid conversation. Observe yourself as a listener in the conversation. Do you look interested? Do you ask good questions? And do you have unconscious body language cues that prevent you from making your desired impact? By looking at yourself, you can often see these quirks right away and develop strategies to address them.

Ask a few trusted colleagues for feedback. There's a difference between what you intended to communicate by how you listen, and what you actually communicated. Do you dominate the conversation? Do you impose your ideas rather than letting people voice their own?

THREE KEYS TO INTENTIONAL LISTENING

Every person is different. Every strategy for becoming a more competent listener will necessarily need time with a professional to iron out unique challenges. However, we can get off to a great start by following three pieces of advice.

1. Forget your ego: This conversation isn't just about you! When we think it's "all about me" we don't listen well.

2. Be the first to give: if you want someone to understand you, take Stephen Covey's advice and try to understand them first. It sounds like a paradox, but authentically and honestly trying to understand someone is the best way to gain influence or buy-in from someone.

3. Ask more and better questions: better questions lead to better answers. By knowing what to ask, you'll gain more information and perspective from other people. And that will allow you to solve problems faster, make better decisions, and move towards your goals more effectively.

BLIND SPOT NINE
Not Planning for Family Emergencies

Prism was looking good. We had Geoff's training to show us how to communicate, and Carrol's advice to show us how to listen. David's insight kept our teams focused. Julie's facilitated sessions made our direct managers engage our staff. Dorothy had helped me own my leadership style, and Dean had made sure everyone was safe at work.

All in all, things were looking up professionally, but the next time I called Cindy, it was to deal with something a lot more personal.

It was just past lunch on a Thursday. I was kneeling on the floor of the company kitchen, fiddling with machine bits. Some of the bits were corkscrewed wire, others were complicated valve pumps, some were anonymous doohickeys—they were all shiny, and smelled faintly of machine oil.

I was sticking a valve to a doohickey when Austin came in with a Tupperware container of spaghetti.

"What's that Russ?" He asked. He sidestepped around the mess and popped his container in the microwave.

"A brand new espresso machine!" I exclaimed. "Not only does it pull a perfect shot, but there are special chambers for brewing macchiatos, americanos, and lattes. It even does tea!"

"And it didn't come fully assembled?" Austin asked. The microwave beeped. He opened the door and pulled out his food. Steam snaked out the open Tupperware lid.

"Well, it did," I admitted. "But I heard there's a way you can fiddle with the steam valve to get a better pull."

Austin nodded. He stepped around me again and pulled out a plate. "I'm more of an instant coffee guy."

"I'm going to pretend I didn't hear that," I said, winking. "Espresso is the perfect blend of science and art."

"Instant coffee requires no mechanical expertise." Austin countered. He dumped his pasta on the plate, stuck a fork through the top, and headed out.

"Russell?"

That was Nancy's voice.

"In here Nancy!" I called.

Nancy came in. She stopped at the entrance. She held out a Blackberry—my Blackberry. "Phone for you." She said. She sounded a little out of breath, like she'd run here.

"Ah yes," I said. I held up my pointer finger. "It's probably David again. Or maybe Cindy. Is it Geoff?"

Nancy closed her eyes. "It's your mother." She said it in a shaky voice.

I looked up. "What?"

Nancy held out the phone. I took it.

"Hello?" I asked. "Mom? What's happen—Mom, why are you crying?"

An hour later, I was at Collingwood Hospital's reception desk.

"Hi," I murmured. "My name is Russell Baxter. I'm here to see Stephen Baxter."

The receptionist opened up the hospital database. "Stephen Baxter... He's on the third floor. Room 381."

"Thanks," I pushed off from the desk and headed to the elevators.

I still couldn't quite believe that I was here. The hospital backdrop: nurses pushing trolleys, blinking medical equipment, bland hospital paintings, all passed by in a blur as I walked through the hallways, looking for room 381.

Finding the room had a dreamy quality to it. I felt unbalanced. I felt like I'd fall, and the floor would swallow me up.

And then I came to room 381, and the world became all too real.

"Oh Dad..." I whispered.

Stephen Baxter, my father, lay on the hospital bed tucked under a thin blue blanket. His eyes were closed. His face indefinably tired. Plastic tubes snaked out of his nose.

My mother and sister sat next to him. Their eyes were red. Their faces wet.

They told me it was a stroke.

My dad had never lived a healthy life. He'd quite smoking years ago, but for two decades, he inhaled a pack a day. For his entire life, he'd eaten close to our Scottish-Canadian roots: lots of fried food, lots of coffee, lots of butter on lots of bagels.

"I found him watching TV," my mom said. "And then I realized something was wrong."

I listened to my mother. I watched my father. His toast-rack chest rose and fell, faintly, and slowly. My mother said his consciousness came and went. Sometimes he was lucid, sometimes he wasn't. Sometimes, he slept, and it was a deep sleep.

"It's important that we see what comes back." My mother said. "The doctors said he could make a full mental recovery. But... He'll probably..."

I knelt carefully on the chair. I felt my mom's hand on my shoulder. I grabbed it, and I cried.

Some unknowable time later, I collected myself and stepped outside to make a call.

"Cindy?" I asked. "We have to cancel that appointment. There's a family emergency. I... I don't know what to do. Well—it's my father."

I ended up spilling my guts to Cindy. And why not? We'd become friends as well as colleagues. I needed a shoulder to cry on.

"I just don't know what to do." I paced a circle in the hallway. An orderly pushed by me with a patient in a wheelchair.

"Are you going to take some time off work?" Cindy asked.

"I guess I'll have to." I said. "I hadn't thought about it."

I leaned against the wall and slid down into a squat. Yes. My father was sick; I had to take time off. But how long could I spare? I drummed my fingers on the phone, thinking. I could spare some time now, maybe hand over the reigns to the senior teams, and let them go on autopilot for a while.

I could manage to take the next two days off. Maybe a week, if I pushed it.

But would a week be long enough? A stroke wasn't like a broken leg or the flu. This was something that lasted. And eventually, I'd have to return to work. My sister, too. And when we did, we'd be leaving our mom all alone, with dad at the hospital.

"I'll take a week," I sighed. "And see what we can do from there."

"You're a great guy, Russell," Cindy said. "And if it's alright by you, I'm going to send someone to talk on your final day off. Her name is Sherri Galler. She might be able to help."

"I don't feel like anything can help me just now." I said sadly. "But sure. Thanks for listening Cindy."

"Take care of yourself Russell."

The next week went. It didn't "go well." It didn't "go bad." It just went. Even now, I can't remember much about it. That week was a movie, with a jerky projector, broken stereo, and badly damaged film. It was all a blur to me, except for some images that lingered in my head like still frames from where the film reel stuck.

I remembered my father waking up, and talking to him. He had difficulty talking, but I heard very clearly that he wanted a shave. I remembered my mother, wandering alone in her house, after my sister finally had to get back to her own job.

And I remembered speaking to Sherri Galler.

I met Sherri on a Friday on the way back from the hospital. Since I was so far away from the office, we just decided to meet up at a Starbucks. It was a rainy day, and I crossed my arms over my head as I ran to the door.

Sherri was the only person in the restaurant. She looked younger than me, with bright blonde hair and a red blazer. She cocked her head as I waved at her from the door.

"Russell Baxter?" She asked. "Sherri Galler. It's nice to finally meet you."

"Sherri." I nodded, and took the opposite seat. "I'm sorry—I'm still a little bit of a mess."

I told Sherri everything that had happened to me lately. It had been a busy week: my sister was practically living at my mother's now, and my mother didn't know what to do with herself. The entire family felt stretched, somehow. I personally felt like I could snap any minute.

I felt distantly like I was embarrassing myself, talking like this. But if I was, Sherri didn't give any indication. She listened to everything I said. Even when I was tripping over my words, backtracking, and in general making a mess of a conversation, she gave off an aura of care that put me at ease.

"And that's how Cindy told me about you," I finished. "I'm sorry—I don't even think I fully know what you do. Cindy mentioned—elder care?"

Sherri folded her hands on our table. "Somewhat. My specialty is working with professionals who have to manage the difficulties that occur when a parent or spouse is ailing."

She continued. "There are a lot of complexities that we just can't plan for in cases like this. As well, we often don't have the ability to leave work indefinitely to care for our parents ourselves."

"I was just thinking about that." I said, rubbing my temples. I was getting a lot more headaches than usual, but I didn't take anything for it. The headaches had taken away a lot of sleep. "I took this week off, and I don't think I'll be able to take another without everyone at my company suffering. But it's hard to just go back to work when your family is in trouble."

Outside, the wind gusted. Someone's newspaper skidded across the parking lot.

"You know." I added. "I just got back from seeing my father. I gave him a shave. No one ever told me that was something I'd have to do."

I remembered how I navigated the razor around the curve of my father's chin, how the cream lopped off the razor as I clinked it against a mug of warm water. I remembered when my dad had first taught me how to shave—that must have been over forty years ago.

I reached for a napkin and dabbed at my eyes. "Sorry. I didn't know about any of this. I mean—I knew on some level that this could happen but... I didn't think this would be so hard."

"We're a lot more emotional than we think," Sherri said. "I've had lawyers, business owners, even religious leaders who have difficulty handling an aging or ailing parent or spouse."

"Right." I said. I put my head in my hands. "So, you're the expert Sherri. What do we do from here?"

"Well," Sherri said, holding her hands together. "Every situation is unique, and each family has its own unique way of coping. But, let's start with your dad. How's he doing?"

I shrugged. "We're still waiting for a final prognosis. But it does look like he'll need extensive care and physical therapy."

"And that's where I'd come in." Sherri said. "I can do some digging, and work out a next step to fit everyone's needs. It's just like any other business solution: what's the problem, what's the goal, what's the solution based on those factors."

Sherri drummed her fingers on the table. "We can start by arranging care for your father at the hospital. And then we can sit in on that family meeting. Your doctors will probably have one very soon."

"I remember them mentioning that." I said.

"And after the doctors give their opinions," Sherri spoke slowly, choosing her words, "If it looks like he can't come home, we'll educate you on the process of that."

"I didn't even think about that," I said. "What would that entail?"

"We'll have to deal with CCAC—that's Community Care Access Centres," she said. "CACC is the government body that places people into long-term care facilities. But they can be tricky, because if you don't follow their rules explicitly, you can be charged, and your dad might not end up in the best place."

I didn't even know the government got involved in cases like this. I looked out the window. "And what about staying at home?" I asked.

"We can look into at-home care, too." Sherri said. "We'll be dealing with CCAC again there, and they'll be providing ADL support—aspects of daily living. But that's the only care that will be provided by the government, and it's only two hours a day. Everything else will require a private company."

"That's a complicated decision." I said.

My phone buzzed in my pocket, startling me. I shot an apologetic look at Sherri and pulled out my cell.

"My mom's calling," I murmured. I debated whether or not to answer, and decided to call her back.

"It's too soon for us to make any decisions now," Sherri said. "First, we'd need to talk more with the rest of your family, and I'd have to do my own research. But, if you want me to go ahead, we'll do the legwork for you. I'll present you with my information, and we can make a decision later."

Sherri smiled, "In the meantime, I suggest you call back your mother."

I smiled. "I think I'll do that."

Over the next few weeks, I stayed in touch with Sherri. She sat with us at the doctor's, and listened as they gave their prognosis: my dad would make a full mental recovery, but he would be paralyzed on his left side. He'd need physiotherapy, and a lot of care.

From there, we talked with him, my mom, and sister. My mother wouldn't hear of sending him outside the house, so the entire family pulled together to provide him with at-home care.

Through it all, Sherri helped us out. She steered us through the procedures, counseled us on what to expect, and in general cleared the way on a journey I never thought I'd have to take.

A month later, I was talking with Sherri about ironing out some home-care options at the office.

"Sherri?" I asked. "I wanted to know, you've helped me out so much. Do you do classes as well?"

"Absolutely." Sherri said. "I run lunch and learn seminars for corporations on topics like ailing parents and spouses, as well as other topics like estate management."

I looked out into the office, and all the people out there. They all had families, like me, and, like me, none of them were immune to tragedy. "I think I'd like to have you come over and talk to everyone. Just knowing that there was a next step, and that when bad things happen, we can use that knowledge to move forward."

"I'd love to come over." Sherri said.

"Super." I said. "Tell you what, why don't you brief me on the subject matter so I can write some notes. Then I'll write up an email for everyone."

NOTES FROM RUSSELL'S WORD DOCUMENT

BAD THINGS DO HAPPEN

That's the simplest, rawest way to say it. Bad things can happen to good people. Unfortunately, it's not a truth we're comfortable with, and it's not something we think about as much as we should. That can leave us unprepared when tragedy does occur.

That's why we need education. Education in the whats, hows, wheres and whys of illness, death, and care can help us move through tragedy and protect us and our loved ones from further harm.

WHEN BAD THINGS HAPPEN, YOUR OTHER RESPONSIBILITIES DON'T EVAPORATE

One person can't do the work of two—not for long. And in the event of illness or death, we can stretch ourselves to a breaking point handling the new responsibilities of tragedy with the responsibilities that don't go away, like our work.

WHEN BAD THINGS HAPPEN, THERE'S PAPERWORK

In Canada, our government provides baseline care to ailing parents and spouses, and also manages the intricacies of inheritance and estate. There's a law for everything, paperwork for everything, and so much red tape it might as well be Christmas.

But when we're already dealing with a personal or family emergency, it isn't easy to navigate the bureaucratic maze. Already knowing what to do, or having someone guide you through the steps, will get you out of that maze faster, and back to your friends, family, and job.

BLIND SPOT TEN
Presenting Without Authenticity

The next two months flew by as I prepared my speech for Prism's annual general meeting.

The AGM was a big event for me. By the time I became the heir apparent for the CEO, I'd shadowed Tim for a year. I'd sat in on meetings, contributed my thoughts, and gradually taken over more and more duties, while Tim had phased himself out. But the AGM was something that had always been Tim's responsibility. And while I'd certainly been to a few meetings, I'd never actually spoken at one.

I was a little nervous.

That's why I left nothing to chance. I finished my writing my opening marks the Thursday before the meeting. When I finished, I gave the speech one final perusal, and hit SAVE, then PRINT.

My desk printer shuddered to life. I grabbed my reading glasses, and when every page had filed out, I tapped the pages, grabbed my ballpoint pen, and ruffled around in my desk drawer. After a few seconds of searching, I found a set of yellow cue cards.

Very carefully, I began to transcribe the printout of my speech to the cards.

This was one of the many presentation tricks I'd picked up over the years. Reading from a piece of white printer paper looked terrible. The paper crinkled, wrinkled, and slipped in my hands. On the other hand, cue cards were sleek and solid—perfect for reading off of during a presentation.

I was on cue card number six when Nancy knocked on my door.

"Hi Nancy." I said. I removed my glasses and blinked. "Everything okay?"

"I think you should give Cindy a call." Nancy said.

"But why?"

Nancy looked at my printouts.

"The speech?" I asked. I held out cue card number six "It's a great speech! I wrote it according to Geoff Weinstein's best principles."

"The speech is *written* well." Nancy said. She leaned against my visitor chair. "But... Maybe someone could help you with the delivery?"

"My delivery?" I asked.

"You have a tendency to read right off the page." Nancy said. "Also, when you're not reading, you keep your hands plastered to your sides like this."

Nancy stuck her hands to her hips.

"But, I'm animated." I insisted. "I—I walk around the room."

"Yes. But you don't move your hands. You look like a penguin." She said.

"Really?" I asked.

I looked down at my hands. They were currently plastered to my sides. Did I really do that when I was presenting?

"I think it'd be a really good idea to get some professional help." Nancy said.

"Well... We can't be too careful. Maybe you're right. I'll call Cindy." I said.

"That's a great idea," Nancy said.

Nancy left. I picked up the phone and dialed for Cindy's office phone; Cindy picked up on the third ring.

I asked if there was anyone she knew who could deliver a session on presentation skills for my entire senior team. I also made an offhand remark on how it would be good to brush up on my own technique as well. Cindy said she'd put her best person on it.

I scheduled a session for myself and the team in two weeks on Monday morning. I called in every member of my senior team who conducted presentations as part of their regular work.

Two weeks later, I drove in to work that Monday, dropped my things in the office, checked my email, and got up to leave for the boardroom, where the presentation would be held. But as I rose, I stopped myself.

"Huh." I said. "I nearly forgot."

I opened my desk drawer, and removed something.

It was a simple notebook. A plain blue spiral one from Staples. It had two hundred and sixty pages.

This notebook was the answer to a long-running problem: since meeting Cindy, I'd had a habit of scribbling down whatever I'd learned from her, or the other members of the Athena alliance. The problem was: these game-changing learning moments had turned into clutter. My office was littered with napkins, brochures, and random printouts. No more. From now on, whenever I learned something new, I'd write it down in this notebook.

Just then, Nancy walked past my door.

"Oh, Nancy!" I called. Nancy turned her head and swung back into the office. "Have you seen the trainer yet?"

"Oh yes, I went and got her." Nancy said. "She's set up everything, and we're just chatting in my office now."

I peeked out of my door as Nancy headed off. Through the open door to Nancy's office, I saw the back of the trainer's head. She was a woman, with very familiar hair.

As I wondered where I'd seen her before, the trainer turned her head. It was Cindy.

"Cindy?" I asked. I came into Nancy's office. "What are you doing here?"

"I told you that I'd send my best person on it, didn't I?" Cindy asked. "I teach presentation skills as part of my work at Athena Training and Consulting Inc.."

We caught up with each other as we walked together to the board room. When we got there, it was exactly time for the presentation to start, and my entire team was seated. I shuffled into the back row, and Cindy took her place at the front of the room.

A Powerpoint slide lit up on the screen behind her. The slide showed the agenda for the meeting.

"Can anyone tell me one of the most-feared things on the planet?" Cindy asked.

I knew this one. I raised my hand. "Public speaking?" I suggested.

"That's right." Cindy said. "So when people attend funerals, *they'd rather be in the box than giving the eulogy.*"

This got a few laughs.

Cindy moved on. She talked about the goals of this presentation: she wanted to teach us to move past nervousness, to structure presentations, and to align our body language, speech patterns, and presentation design, to inform our audience.

As she spoke, Cindy moved through a few slides. In every slide, she kept the text to a minimum. Somehow, this actually increased their value. I found myself listening more to her, than trying to read every word on the slide.

"We're afraid of public speaking." Cindy said. "We're afraid because we fear we'll make a mistake, or forget what to say, or look foolish."

I nodded to myself. Most of my staff followed the same template in presentations: they read slides, and distributed massive handouts. No one innovated. It was almost like they were afraid of deviating from the norm.

Cindy pressed on. "There is no one golden ticket, silver bullet, or bronzed ideal that we have to follow. I believe presenting can be done in a number of different ways, as long as it's authentic, professional and relevant."

"Some people think that you're not supposed to smile too much in a professional presentation." Cindy said. To demonstrate, she pulled her face into a blank slate.

"Or make eye contact," she dropped her eyes to the floor.

"Or move." She stiffened her shoulders, clapped her hands down and—for a moment—looked very much like a penguin.

Cindy brought her head up. Her smile returned. Her arms relaxed and she took a few careful steps around the room. The heads in the room turned to follow her. She had our complete attention. "And some people think that you should do all of those things, even if they're not authentic to you."

Cindy came back to the middle of the room. "I say that you should do anything that works within your natural style."

At this point, Cindy invited a few people up. She encouraged them to give a small speech on whatever they felt like. As each person went up, she invited the rest of us to offer feedback on how they moved, spoke, and ultimately made their point.

It was working well. Everyone in this room knew each other. We trusted each other's opinions, and were able to give feedback without being too soft, or too hard. The exercise also let us reflect on our own behavior: when we were about to call out a presenter on talking too fast, or on holding poor posture, we were forced to consider if we did that as well.

Cindy ended the exercise with a round of applause for the presenters. She remarked that each presenter had their own personal attributes, and that they could include these attributes into their presentation style.

"Take me for instance." Cindy said, pointing to herself. "I'm a very friendly type of person, and so I try to be more casual in my presentation. But just because that works for me, doesn't mean it will necessarily work for you. Instead, you should do what is authentic for you. Once you've developed your personal style, you can plan your presentation accordingly. Use your natural attributes to enhance your presentation, not fit into some paradigm."

I rubbed my chin thoughtfully. Cindy was right. Her presentation was frank, open, and charming; a perfect representation of the Cindy I'd come to know. And as a result, I found myself responding more to her lesson.

That was an interesting thought: I liked Cindy, and the qualities she exuded on a personal level. She'd made a congruency between that personality, her verbal communication, and her nonverbal communication. That congruency carried the qualities I liked about Cindy into her presentation.

I'd sat through a lot of meetings. I'd led a lot of boring meetings. I was going through those presentations acting a role—acting like I thought a project manager should, or a department head, or a CEO—instead of going through a presentation as me, and using my best qualities.

"Essentially," Cindy said. "Before you start preparing for your speech, realize what assets you can *use*, realize what your audience *needs*, and bring them together."

"From there," Cindy said. "We can actually start our work."

"When planning a presentation, I approach it as an entire experience." Cindy said. She waved her hand across the room. "Your speech isn't just about standing up, saying a bunch of facts, and then sitting down. You have to work a golden thread—a consistency, or congruency—into your message. One of the simplest ways is the old southern preacher method:

tell 'em what you're gonna tell them, tell 'em, then tell 'em what you told 'em. Structure your speech so your audience remembers the message."

I pinched the bridge of my nose, remembering the speech I'd written. I'd completely forgotten to use that simple trick.

"But your presentation goes beyond just the words." Cindy continued. "When I say it's an entire experience, I mean everything. From what lighting you're using, to what gestures you'll make, to whether or not you have handouts given before, during, or after the presentation."

"By the way," Cindy said. "Notice how I didn't give you handouts this time. But there will be some by the table as you leave."

This got a few more chuckles. When the room was quiet again, Cindy resumed her talk.

"What I've just said is an introduction. To change the way you might think about presenting, and how we can look at it differently to engage our audiences. Now, we'll go over specific techniques, like vocal variation and breathing techniques."

"But." Cindy raised her hand. "Before I do that, I'm going to give you one tip. If you follow this tip, you'll be able to leave the room right now, and still do a much better job at presenting."

Cindy looked around the room. She leaned forward, and said, quietly, but clearly: "Practice."

The word echoed in the silent room. Cindy straightened back up.

"Presentation is a learned skill. You get better at skills by practicing. Again and again and again." Cindy said. "Practice in front of the mirror. Practice in front of a person you trust. Practice while you imagine the crowd responding in front of you."

Someone raise their hand. "Is practicing in front of a mirror so we can check our body language?"

"Exactly." Cindy agreed. "The words we speak only represent seven percent of how your message is heard. Fifty-five percent is nonverbal, and thirty-eight percent is in vocal tone. Keeping this in mind, you can understand the importance of practicing both what you are going to say and how you are going to say it. You need to get up and actually practice all the aspects of your presentation—not just read off a screen. This is where I have found most people have not spent adequate time, and as a result, they end up lacking confidence once they are in front of an audience."

Cindy concluded her introduction. "Be wary of memorization. At most, I'd recommend memorizing your first few sentences, because that's when you'll be most nervous. But you should never ever, ever memorize your entire presentation."

Now Cindy ventured into the nuts and bolts of presentations. She showed us how to vary our gestures according to room and audience size, including prompting gestures to evoke responses, emphatic gestures to underscore a point, and suggestive gestures to guide the audience's thoughts along our narrative. She taught us how to breathe. She taught us how to inflect our sentences: to dip and dive along our words to captivate audiences and keep them hooked. She covered the before, the after, and everything in between of how to make an amazing presentation.

Halfway through, I realized I'd better take some notes. I patted my pocket, and realized I'd forgotten my new notebook on my desk.

I did find something though: a hard corner in my back pocket. I reached in and pulled the thing out.

It was a blank cue card.

Smirking at myself, I clicked my pen, and started taking notes. I filled up the cue card, front and back, when Cindy was ready to end the lesson.

"Now, I would like to end our session today with another exercise." Cindy said. "And I'll need the help of Prism's CEO."

I stopped writing.

I looked up.

Cindy gave a big smile. "Come on up, Russell."

I sheepishly got to my feet. A few people laughed and clapped.

"We're going to go through the same feedback exercise we tried at the start of the session." Cindy said. "The only difference is, we're going to see the difference that these tips can make. You've all seen Russell present before, and now we can see the difference they can make."

I gulped. This was a little bit petrifying. These were my coworkers: what was at stake if I made a fool of myself? I felt hot. I worried if I was blushing. I looked terrible when I blushed.

But hadn't Cindy taught us somewhere down the line how to deal with nervousness? I thought back to the cue card.

One of the tips had been to stand straight. Chest out. Head high. I tried the posture. Cindy was still talking, so the attention was on her. I took some deep breaths. I began to feel better.

"Take it away, Russell." Cindy said. I got some more scattered applause, and that put me more at ease.

I began to speak.

It wasn't perfect. My gestures were a bit clunky. My modulations and inflections went through a bit stilted. But beneath that, there was something new in how I spoke. There was a ghost of flavor to my words, a vitality that hadn't been there before.

I finished my short speech. The entire room clapped. I think Nancy whistled.

I took a little bow, and stepped back to my seat. Cindy wrapped up her presentation, and the session adjourned. I pocketed the cue card on my seat. I went to talk with Cindy, and promised myself that it was the last cue card I'd ever use.

NOTES FROM RUSSELL'S CUE CARD

GOOD PRESENTATIONS USE CONGRUENT ELEMENTS

A presentation is more than just saying the right words. It's about being your personal best. This performance hinges on congruency: making sure how you look, how you speak, and what you say, is aligned with your intent for the presentation.

When we prepare for a presentation, too often we focus solely on our words. We don't practice delivery, and we don't wonder about the time, place, or mood of the audience. But, we can harness these elements to empower a presentation.

EASY WAYS TO ENGAGE AN AUDIENCE

Use a golden thread. It's not enough to just ramble on in a presentation, you have to connect everything you do in a certain flow. A strong opening and closing are vital, as are that congruency we talked about earlier.

Ask questions. Genuine or rhetorical questions can quickly grasp an audience's attention. It brings them into an engaged role with the presenter, as opposed to being passive observers in the presentation.

Minimize distractions. Think of the setup of your room—does it focus audience attention on you? Think of when you'll give handouts—will people start reading ahead and divert their attention from you?

Go minimal for Powerpoint. If a picture is worth a thousand words, then one slide is worth eight minutes of talking. Instead of overloading your slides with transcripts from your speech, use them as visual aides to highlight your points. A good rule of thumb is to have a maximum of eight words per line, eight lines per slide and one point on every slide.

Be comfortable. You don't have to be Tony Robbins, just be your authentic self. If you try to be someone you're not, the audience will sense it, and they'll disengage from your message.

PRACTICE

When you need to prepare for a presentation, practice your speech and gestures, but also rehearse mentally. Imagine yourself going up to the podium, and delivering your lines.

Mental rehearsal, paired with physical practice, is a powerful tool: Olympic athletes use it to win medals! Mental rehearsal works wonders. Your unconscious brain can't tell the difference between what you imagine and what actually happens; that means that by visualizing your presentation, you'll naturally be more comfortable when you get up to speak. Subconsciously, you'll already have done it before!

While you practice, steer away from rote memorization. Instead, know your key points, lines, and figures, and then use your script as a guideline. This way, you can always rework your words on the fly, or deal with a sudden disturbance. This will also allow you the freedom to improvise: you'll be able incorporate any relevant information or activities that occur during your presentation, such as referring to something that might have happened in the room.

BLIND SPOT ELEVEN
Selling Without Understanding Needs

It was three weeks after the AGM. I ambled over to my office with a small smile on my face. I felt good. The AGM had gone great, and I'd also conveniently scheduled a two-week vacation immediately following the meeting. Today was my first day back.

The trip had done wonders. I was relaxed. I was clear-minded. I was *tanned*. Of course, while on vacation, my internet connection had been pretty shoddy, but that wasn't so bad. For two whole weeks, I hadn't thought about work at all.

"Welcome back Russell." Austin said. "Nice tan."

"Thanks Austin." I waved as I walked by his cubicle.

"Hey!" Dennis said as I entered the main hall. "Good to see you Russell! How was the trip?"

"Bali was beautiful." I said.

"Did you get us chocolate?" Tina asked as she passed by.

"In the kitchen." I said. "See you guys later."

As I sat down at my desk, my cell beeped. I had a text from Cindy. *Welcome back! Still on for today?*

"Oh, I nearly forgot." I muttered to myself. I'd scheduled a meeting with Cindy for the first day of my return. I wanted to set up a training program to help our project managers manage their time better.

That's right, I texted back. *See you soon?*

I got a reply a few minutes later. *On my way already. I'll be at your front door in five minutes.*

Four minutes later I got up to meet Cindy at the foyer. Nancy stopped me at the door.

"Russell?" Nancy said. "We need to talk about Craig."

"That's right!" I slapped my palm. "You and Craig sent me a bunch of emails while I was on vacation! But my internet was so spotty I never ended up reading any of them. Where is Craig anyway? I had a meeting scheduled with him today."

"He didn't come in today." Nancy said.

"Oh." I said. "Well, where is he?"

"Australia."

"Australia." I repeated.

"Yes." Nancy said. "With his mother in Adelaide."

Suddenly those emails made a lot more sense; Craig had probably found some super-cheap tickets to Australia, and decided to make a last-minute trip to see his mother. He and Nancy had probably sent all those emails because they wanted to let me know before I got back.

"Well," I said. "I of all people can't blame anyone for going on vacation. When's he coming back?"

"He's not." Nancy said.

I squinted. "… Okay?"

"It's his father." Nancy said. "He—he passed away, very suddenly."

"Oh."

I stared blankly at Nancy. "Oh" was all I could say. Then, Nancy's words sunk in slowly, like ice water.

"Oh no." I said.

Nancy went on: Craig's father had been battling prostate cancer for a number of years. His condition had worsened suddenly in the past month, and two weeks ago…

"He wants to stay with his mother and look after her and the rest of the family." Nancy said. "He's coming back in a week to collect his things, but he'll just be dealing with immigration, his furniture, selling his apartment…"

"So, our lead sales manager is gone?" I asked.

"Looks like it." Nancy said.

I felt a curious mix of emotions. Of course, if Craig thought moving back to Adelaide was the best choice, then I wouldn't dream of stopping him; my own family was still dealing with the aftermath of my father's stroke. I knew what it felt like to look after your family, and watch it be torn by tragedy.

And yet, a small, selfish part of me was nervous about the company.

I took a long, calming breath. Remember the sea breeze. Remember the hot sand on your feet. Remember the pretty girls serving drinks.

"Hang on a sec." I said. I turned away from Nancy and headed down the hall.

"Where are you going?" Nancy asked.

"First, I am going to talk to Cindy." I said. "And then, I am going to hyperventilate for a few minutes."

I found Cindy waiting at the foyer. She gave me a warm smile, but it turned into a look of concern as I came closer.

"Cindy," I said. "I'm so sorry, but a situation just came up. I don't know if we're going to be able to have that talk."

"What's up?" She asked.

She sat me down in one of the chairs. I explained what Nancy had just told me.

"Wow, that is serious." Cindy commented. "Are you going to manage okay?"

"I'm not sure." I said, honestly. "Well, I guess that's one less meeting to attend today."

"What was the meeting for?" Cindy asked.

"I wanted to talk to Craig about expanding our sales team globally, with a virtual infrastructure to stay connected." I sighed. "I thought it would help us in the next big sales push."

For a second, Cindy looked lost in thought. She checked her phone. I saw her scroll through her calendar for the day. She nodded to herself, and stood up.

"Well, first things first." She said, "Your manager—you said his name was Craig?—he's doing something important to him. We can understand why he needs to leave. Are there any candidates who could fill in on an interim position?"

"Yes." I said, thinking on it. "Nancy would know better, but I think we have a few people who could fill in."

"Alright." Cindy said. "So you might be able to start interviewing as soon as next week. And, while you look for a full replacement, I can come in and tune up your team. That way, when you get a new manager, they'll have a dynamite team to work with."

"What do you mean?" I asked.

"I'm a sales trainer as well." Cindy said. She picked up her purse and slung it over her shoulder. "I also have several other sales trainers and coaches in my alliance, and feel pretty confident we can support you in this initiative."

I grinned. As usual, Cindy had my back. I stood up as well. "Where do we start?" I asked.

Cindy held out her phone. "I have some free time this Thursday. Would that time work for you?"

It did. That Thursday, Cindy came back to the office. I went out to meet her myself.

"Morning Cindy." I said, rubbing my palms together. "Ready to get started? How can we start boosting our sales?"

"Well, first let's head over to sales," Cindy said. "I'll listen in on a few calls, look at your sales process, examine your previous training material, and check out your policies."

"That sounds great." I said. I added, apologetically. "Thanks, by the way. I know this was slightly short notice."

"It's all good." Cindy brushed away my concern. "I live for this."

On the way over to the sales cubicles, I explained my current understanding—or lack thereof—of the sales team.

"The thing is, I've never performed in a sales function, so sometimes I don't know what to look out for." I said. "I've always known that it's an environment where you need continuous learning and coaching, but I've always left it up to my sales managers to know how the team should be developed."

"You've got it right, Russell." Cindy held out her hand. "Good sales are the result of learning. The way I teach it, good sales come down to finding out about your customer's needs through a skilled salesperson asking great questions. Ultimately, these skills directly correlate to the success of your business. And not paying attention to your sales models spells trouble."

"I agree with you on that one," I said as we neared the cubicles.

"Now, you don't sell directly to consumers, right?" She asked.

"That's right. Our clients are the distributors." I said. "They put our appliances in retail stores, and then customers buy them."

We came to the sales team: a huddle of ten people, each doing their thing in as much peace and quiet as a cubicle could afford. Cindy looked over them. With me, we pulled aside some of them to answer a few of her questions, which ranged from how they liked to follow up with clients, to how they interacted with Craig, to how they pitched our products to distributors. Cindy even shadowed a call.

Afterwards, Cindy and I headed to cafeteria. I poured us both coffee, and we discussed the team.

"The way I see it," Cindy said, stirring some sugar into her cup, "There aren't any huge worries with your staff. They're perfectly competent, and have a good sales attitude. That being said, I can see a few avenues to improve how they sell."

"Well you're the expert." I said. "What do we do?"

"This is a problem that I've found in a lot of sales teams." Cindy said. "When I was listening in to those calls, it sounded like your team was just trying to sell a product."

She sipped her coffee. "Hey, this is *good*."

"Isn't selling a product their job?" I asked.

"Yes, but not all of it." Cindy said. "You can drive sales higher by having them cross-sell and up-sell. Prism offers many different appliances. And from what I could tell, not all your distributors carry all your products. We need to look into why this is, and train your sales reps to sell differently to those distributors who could carry additional appliances."

"But isn't that a bit like those used car salesmen?" I asked. "The ones who try to get you to pay more for their own gain?"

"Not when you do it right." Cindy pointed out. "Effective cross-selling and up-selling starts by learning about clients, and what *they* want and need. After you learn that, you match their needs to products and services you can offer. It's a win-win. They find answers to a problem, and you make the sale. In fact my experience has been if you clearly understand your client's needs and propose a solution that will provide a solution to those needs, *the customer closes the sale themselves*."

"Well, that makes sense." I admitted. "I definitely agree that bombarding clients with information won't close a sale. It's never worked on me, after all."

"That's right." Cindy agreed. "In fact, it's usually the bad salespeople who end up talking a lot. A good salesperson actually doesn't do a lot of talking: they ask great questions."

"So, how do you start asking good sales questions?" I asked.

"Well, every situation is unique, and after learning some more about Prism, I'll be able to suggest other sales processes." Cindy said. "But one model I like is called SPIN."

Cindy folded her hands over the table. "SPIN is a sales process for asking relevant questions. These questions are designed to help the client discover how your products can help them. The name is an acronym that stands for Situation, Problem, Implication, and Needs-payoff. Those are the types of questions you ask when using SPIN. It's an old model by a man named Neil Rakham, but I love it because it still works."

"Sounds dynamite." I said.

"It is." Cindy said. "There's a certain power in the right question at the right time. You can manage people by asking questions effectively and influence their decisions. I'll work with your sales team to develop a series of SPIN questions for your prospects and clients."

Cindy continued. "But the ultimate benefit of questions is that you get to know your clients on a deeper level. And that leads to another advantage."

I hazarded a guess. "Lasting friendships?"

"Those are great, but what I'm talking about are referrals." Cindy rubbed her thumb and forefinger together. "I personally think it's bad form to ask for referrals before you've built up a good relationship and have worked successfully with your client. But once they trust you, then why not?"

Cindy drained the last of her coffee. "Now, there are of course other ways I think we could augment your sales staff and their skills. We could talk about mindfulness, goal-setting, and strategies for closing. But, unfortunately I've got to get to another meeting soon. So, let me share one last insight that I think could be very helpful."

"I'm all ears." I said, leaning forward.

"You need someone to fill in for Craig's position," Cindy said. "Now, that's an area that's Nancy's specialty. She'll probably be looking for someone outside the company, and someone who has a strong sales background, familiarity with virtual teams, and who has strong coaching skills. With that being said, when the new manager is on board, if you need any additional coaching or support I have lots of resources to draw from."

"I hadn't even thought about coaching skills." I said. "Sales managers just have to manage, don't they?"

"Ah, you've found the problem." Cindy insisted. "Effective sales managers coach salespeople to deliver their own success. But when you have someone that doesn't understand how to do that, or doesn't understand a sales environment, you're not going to set up an environment for optimal sales."

"I see." I said. "So it's a bit like what David Boyce was talking about with customer service. Everyone needs to be contributing to the ultimate goal of sales—just in a different role."

I continued. "And when you have someone who doesn't know much about sales at the top, it will affect the overall operations."

"More or less." Cindy agreed. "When your managers turn into coaches, it'll empower your sales people to do their jobs. I think it'd be best to work with Nancy and look externally."

"Sounds good." I said. "Now, I have a question for you: when we do get someone to fill in for Craig, can you come in and talk to the entire sales team about how to ask great questions?"

Cindy laughed. "I'll see what I can do."

After Cindy left, I hung around the kitchen some more, eating the chocolates I brought back.

On my third chocolate, Nancy came in for coffee. I vaguely remembered I should take some notes on what Cindy had said.

"Hey Nancy. Do you have a napkin or anything?" I asked. "Any paper at all?"

"Well, there's this." Nancy held out the paper bottom for the box of chocolates I'd gotten from Bali.

I shrugged. "You know what? That'll work great."

NOTES FROM RUSSELL'S PAPER

GOOD SALESPEOPLE ASK QUESTIONS

Good sales aren't about picking up the phones and talking; good sales are about asking great questions, listening to the client, and then helping them discover how your products and services can help them.

Neil Rakham's SPIN model is one mode of selling by asking questions. In SPIN selling, the salesperson lets the client do the talking by asking questions. These questions begin by understanding the client's situation, learning about the client's problem, finding out the implications of that problem, and then discovering the payoff that they would receive from buying your product. Throughout this period, the client voices their concerns, and comes to their own conclusions about buying. Since a client naturally trusts an opinion they arrive at themselves more, this makes for a powerful selling tool!

EDUCATE YOUR STAFF ALL THE WAY UP

Your entire sales team, from top to bottom, exists to sell your product. As such, your entire team needs to be geared towards that goal.

Sales is a unique business practice, and managers need insight into that practice to drive sales. Salespeople benefit more from coaching than from managing. A manager can say "go make this many sales" but a coach can fire up their staff, driving them to complete their task. By giving your senior staff management and coaching training, you'll give them superior tools to manage your sales staff, and to coach them to achieve more results.

BALANCE THE WORK ENVIRONMENT

Most people assume that salespeople are lone wolves—out for themselves and no one else. Sometimes this is the case, but mostly it's not: sales teams can benefit greatly from a mixture of competitive and collaborative work environments. Find a way to create a supportive environment that also encourages individual success.

BLIND SPOT TWELVE
Not Engaging Your Remote Workers

"Russell? Did you figure out Communicator?" Nancy asked.

"I think so!" I called back.

I was sitting at my desk with my laptop open in front of me. I pressed a few buttons, and the main screen for Skype popped up on my computer. Done.

I turned my gaze to the heap of tangled wires in front of me.

"Alright then…" I whispered to myself. "The mic feed goes in here… and the headset plug goes in here."

I plugged the wires into my computer, and adjusted a brand-new, space-age headset over my ears. I rolled my shoulders and cricked my neck.

I was a little nervous about today. I had a meeting with a new group of salespeople. The only issue was that none of them were in the office.

Now that Cindy had ironed out our training and protocol for sales, I wanted Prism to make one final leap: I wanted to go international. I wanted Prism microwaves heating popcorn in Japan, Prism refrigerators chilling ice tea in America, and Prism stoves cooking bangers and mash in the UK.

To start our global domination of the low-energy kitchen appliances market, I'd laid the groundwork for gradual expansion. I wanted to move sales into the northern United States, and reach further west into Canada. To make headway in those areas, I wanted salespeople specially placed to take advantage of those markets.

These virtual employees would be self-motivated, autonomous team members that would lead sales in their home states and provinces. It seemed like a good idea. We wouldn't have to expand our office space, for one.

Our new sales manager, Mark, was supposed to manage the virtual employees, but I'd arranged to call each of the salespeople and introduce them to the company myself. It was an odd thing for a CEO to do, but this was such a novel enterprise that I wanted to be on the front line.

I was also a bit nervous. Now that I was about to make the call, I found myself a bit antsy about the long-term future of virtual work. Maybe this was too good to be true. Maybe the successful work-from-home salesperson was a fairy tale.

I was about to find out.

I hit CALL.

"Hello?" A woman's voice came through my headphones.

"Hi Tania," I fiddled with the mic, and adjusted it just level with my chin. "This is Russell Baxter."

"Hi Russell! It's great to meet you."

Tania was our salesperson in Pennsylvania. On paper, she seemed like a great candidate. Nancy had sent her straight through to second-tier interviews. But, while I trusted Nancy and Mark's judgment in hiring her, something seemed off as I talked to her.

I instructed Tania about Prism, my goals for the company, and how the sales team worked. She didn't contribute much to the discussion, but I did hear the tapping of her keyboard.

"Is that—are you writing an email?" I said. "It's kind of distracting."

"Oh, I am—I'm sorry. It's regarding work, I just, I wanted to introduce myself to Mark."

"That's super," I said. "But can it wait until later?"

I hung up a few minutes later. My call with Tania was quick and left a lot to be desired. I was hoping I'd get to know her a little better. But I quickly shrugged it off. Intimate talks usually require some kind of pre-existing rapport, or relationship, and it's obvious she and I didn't have that. Was it even possible to build a relationship when I couldn't see her?

This bothered me all morning. I sensed this could pose a problem, so I made a phone call.

"Hey Cindy. Any chance you could connect me with a virtual business consultant?"

I was waiting for her to swat down my suggestion and tell me there was no such thing. But to my delight, I was wrong.

"I know the perfect person," Cindy said. "I'll have her call you right away."

An hour later, as I was returning to the office after a hardy lunch, my cell rang.

"Hi there, is this Russell Baxter?"

"Speaking." I dashed inside the building to catch the elevator.

"It's Claire Sookman. Cindy told me you're having trouble integrating a new virtual team member."

"Yes, somewhat," I said. "Our company has hired a team of international salespeople to broaden Prism's influence. But recently I made a test call with our new salesperson from Pennsylvania, and it didn't go too well."

"What'd you think went wrong?" Claire asked.

I stepped out of the elevator and headed towards my office. I had a meeting to attend in ten minutes, and wanted to grab a file from my briefcase.

"She didn't seem focused on what I was saying," I said. "She was multitasking, typing an email. Our communication just seemed… disconnected. She also seemed edgy—maybe she was nervous. I might be rambling, is this making sense?"

"Absolutely," Claire said. "I can definitely help you get a handle on this."

"Great," I said. I entered my office, opened up my briefcase, and withdrew the file I needed. "So could you swing by the office sometime today?"

"I could," Claire said. "Or we can do this virtually and discuss it over the phone. It's really up to you."

I paused for a moment. "I think it'd be best if I meet with you in person."

I headed over to the boardroom. It was bustling with members of the marketing department. "Does four o'clock sound okay?" I said, before entering the mayhem.

After a brief meeting, some emails, and a late-afternoon in-house client presentation, I was back in my office. It was four o'clock, and I was awaiting Claire's arrival.

Out my window, an amber sun tucked its torso behind the tops of buildings. A knock at the door shook me out of my daydream.

"Come in!" I called.

Larissa escorted Claire into my office, and dropped a stack of printouts on my desk. "Regarding the new prototypes," she said, and had me sign for approval before taking off.

"Sorry I couldn't meet with you earlier," I said.

"Not a problem," Claire said, sitting down. "Nice to meet you, Russell."

We shook hands. Claire had short brown hair, some funky horn-rimmed glasses, and a big smile.

After talking for several minutes, I found myself getting heated with the same frustration that plagued me this morning.

"Tania's an exceptional worker," I said. "But as I was talking, she started typing an email. There's another thing too—I think she felt uncomfortable, maybe even disengaged."

"Well," Claire said. "We don't know enough right now to say, but it's certainly possible. Actually, it's pretty common for virtual workers to feel disengaged. And, sometimes, this is caused by weak interpersonal relationships. Because, you see, a virtual team is not only task-related, but also socio-emotional."

"Could you repeat that?" I asked. "I studied marketing you see."

Claire leaned forward. "What I mean is: in virtual work, it's just as important for your team members to build strong relationships as it is to have them perform at a high level."

I rubbed the back of my neck. "But why go through the trouble of building relationships? I thought bringing on virtual workers would erase the need for any extra social interaction."

"Well," Claire said. "It really brings everybody together and gets them comfortable, making it much easier for such a geographically dispersed team to get tasks done."

"I see your point," I said. "Especially if it contributes to our bottom line. But I wouldn't even know where to start."

"Look at it like this," Claire said. "To build strong relationships, you need to work on two levels: a 'work' level, and a 'personal' level. To build relationships on a 'work' level, you must be mindful of your communication style. Let me ask you: was your conversation a back-and-forth exchange, or more of a formal briefing?"

"I did most of the talking," I said, shrugging. "There was a lot to discuss."

Claire drummed her fingers on the desk. "That might be the problem right there."

She stood up and walked over to the white board. "Do you mind?" she asked, and uncapped a red marker.

"Please," I nodded, and joined her at the board.

Claire drew two stick people and, in-between them, a one-way arrow. She wrote 'one-way communication.'

"Think back to college," Claire said, pivoting towards me. "When your professor lectured the class—instead of engaging everybody in a lively, collaborative discussion—you probably felt disconnected to your professor and the material, right? Now imagine you were listening to the same lecture through a phone call. Imagine how much *more* bored and detached you'd feel."

She began to draw Z's all over. "I don't know about you, but I'd sure fall asleep."

I chuckled. She was right. I recounted the numerous mind-numbingly boring business lectures I had to sit through to get my degree.

"Here's what you can do," Claire said. She erased the Z's and drew a two-way arrow.

"Focus on 'two-way communication.' Constantly get feedback. View things from your team's perspective. Think of virtual meetings as a two-way conversation, not a one-way lecture."

I rubbed my chin and thought about this.

"Sometimes it's better to just listen," Claire said. "It's a fundamental part to communicating effectively, especially virtually."

That word, listening, rang a bell. I remembered Carrol talking about the importance of intentional listening.

"I was stressed out this morning," I said. "I didn't have the patience to listen to Tania. I was rushed—there was so much to get done."

"Well," Claire said. "That could explain why you and Tania felt so disconnected. Think about it. When we're stressed, we tend to be snappier, tenser, and more impatient than usual, right?"

"Right," I said. I leaned my back against the whiteboard and folded my arms.

"And since Tania couldn't read your body language, she may have thought your frustration as with *her*."

"Are you suggesting I suppress my stress?" I asked.

"Not exactly," Claire said. "It's about being open about how you're feeling. In the virtual world, it's crucial how your communication is perceived. So you need to be authentic and transparent; let your teammates know when you're stressed, or having a bad day. It'll prevent them from misinterpreting your words, your tone of voice, your intentions, and from carrying this negative baggage over to their work."

I nodded and stood up straight. If I want our global sales team to perform well, our communication needs to be open and clear.

Claire lifted her arm towards the door. "Why don't we take a walk?" she asked.

I followed Claire to the sales cubicles, where we leaned against a wall.

"So many people believe that social relationships are impossible to build in a virtual environment where you rarely see each other face-to-face. But I disagree! It's easy to recreate virtually what you're seeing right now."

She nodded towards a group of sales staff laughing and chatting around their cubicles.

"This is precisely how you build relationships on a *personal* level," Claire said.

"With more gossip?" I asked.

Claire chuckled. "Actually—yes! Gossip, talking about sports, or even chatting about the weekend. Basically, you want to get to know the *personal* side of your teammates—their hobbies and interests—instead of only knowing them for, say, their skillsets."

I looked closer. The sales folks were all smiles. They truly looked happy in each other's presence.

I reflected on my talk with Tania. She mentioned she wanted to reach out to Mark, and I shut it down. I didn't even realize how isolated and overwhelmed she might have been feeling.

"Sounds helpful," I mused. "I'll make sure to shoot you an email to learn more about this. Tell you what, let me take a few notes on this."

Claire and I walked back to my office. I pulled out my notebook—the one I hadn't had a chance to use yet—and opened it to a blank page.

"Now where's my pen," I said, digging through my pockets. I plucked a pen out of the bundle of stationary at the far end of my desk, and felt something knock against my elbow.

I'd just spilled coffee all over my new notebook.

I sighed and looked at Claire. I tore some tissues out of a box and mopped up the spill. The only clean piece of paper left was an unused T4 tax form.

"Well, I can do my taxes later," I said.

NOTES FROM RUSSELLL'S T4 FORM

WHY VIRTUAL TEAMS?

With the world becoming increasingly connected and globalized, the need for work to be done face-to-face is diminishing. And with the evolution of technology, it's cheaper and easier than ever to hold a virtual meeting and conduct business from around the world.

ENGAGE VIRTUAL WORKERS ON A PERSONAL LEVEL

Virtual teams have a downside. If nobody initiates social interaction or makes an effort to build enduring relationships, it's easy for employees to become disengaged. Think about how isolated and disconnected a virtual team member can feel from the rest of the team!

The solution is to build more intimate relationships with your teammates. Although work-related chatter is important, it's necessary to get to know the *personal* side of your colleagues.

You can do this by making room for small talk. On special occasions, such as welcoming a new team member, you can arrange virtual pizza parties—just have pizza delivered to your team at lunchtime, and for those in a different time zone, send them a gift certificate for their local coffee shop. Gestures such as these will make everyone feel like an integral part of the team.

You can even play games to kick off a meeting, such as posting a map of the world and asking your team members to use a pointer tool—available with many web conferencing tools—to pinpoint their location. Engaging in any kind of game or activity gets team members involved in pre-meeting discussions.

Your associates will reciprocate your persistent attempt to get to know them better by being more interested in *you*.

USE TWO-WAY COMMUNICATION

It's also important to be mindful of how you interact with your colleagues on work-related issues. Poor, one-way interaction will only alienate them and diminish the potential for interpersonal trust.

Instead, use the "two-way" communication method. Get everybody involved by bringing them into the discussion. Constantly get feedback. For example, you could start meetings by asking your teammates to share one success they've had or one challenge they've faced since the last meeting.

Make a habit going around the virtual meeting room and engaging everybody's thinking. Encourage brainstorming, ask questions, and urge your teammates to share their points of view—whether they agree or disagree with this or that.

By doing this, you're letting your team know you care about their input. You're not asking questions to be polite; you're genuinely interested in their thoughts and ideas. With this communication style, stronger social bonds, comfort, and trust will naturally blossom, and participation and enthusiasm will pour out.

BE AUTHENTIC

When you're geographically separated from your team members, it's important to communicate as authentically and openly as possible. As a manager, you don't want to be an unknown quantity; it'll only cause your teammates to be frustrated and confused as they struggle to interpret your true intentions.

Instead, make your intentions and expectations loud and clear, and don't leave room for misunderstanding. Make sure to lead by example; when you say you're going to do something, do it. Always be open with your colleagues, letting them know when you're having a bad day, so they don't associate your temper with themselves.

Your honesty, your openness, your sharp expectations and clear communication, will gain your teammates' trust.

Epilogue

"From there, everything went pretty smoothly." Russell finished.

It was much later in the day now. There was a slight chill to the air.

Russell and Amir were alone on the bench. The other lunchtime wanderers had left. It was quiet. The only noise came from the birds, and a squirrel scrabbling up a tree.

"There were more challenges, of course." Russell continued. "There always are. But after meeting Cindy, I had resources—no, more than resources—I had friends that I could turn to when I was unsure of what to do. The company expanded, our sales increased, and pretty soon we needed two more plants to keep up with all our orders. I even found us a lovely office complex downtown."

Russell paused. He looked at his watch. "Wow, will you look at the time. Hey, Amir, what do you say we go get a quick bite to eat?"

"I remember that," Amir said distantly. "I remember Claire, I mean. You brought her in a few years ago. It was to brush up on our telecommunications skills."

"Yep." Russell said. "And our virtual sales infrastructure benefited the company nicely. We were one of the first people in our industry to do it."

Russell put his hands on his knees and pushed himself up.

"I've got to spend some more time on the treadmill." He huffed. "That's one thing I'm looking forward to in retirement. That, setting up a garden, and watching MMA fights with my wife."

"A worthy goal." Amir said absently. He was still thinking about the story, and why Russell had called him outside here to hear it.

"I remember ten years ago, when George Saint-Pierre was still in the game." Russell said. "You should have seen him! Pow! Knocked out Hughes with a Superman punch. Amazing."

Amir got up and brushed the seat of my pants. "Thanks for the story, Russell," he said.

"Well, it's your story now." Russell replied. He suddenly sounded quieter, a bit more solemn. "Actually…"

Russell put one hand on his back, bracing it slightly, and bent down to pick up his briefcase. He flicked the latches off the case, and pulled out a journal.

"I wanted to give you this." He said.

The journal was a work of art. It was bound in dark brown leather, with a single rawhide strap wrapped around to clasp it shut. Russell handed the journal to Amir. The words BLIND SPOTS were engraved on the top corner.

Amir undid the rawhide clasp and opened the first page. It was blank.

"You're going to discover your own blind spots in the future." Russell said. "And if I've learned anything, you'll need a place to keep them. Someplace better than old napkins and cue cards."

"This is incredible." Amir whispered. "Russell, thank you."

Russell shrugged. He cocked his head back to the office—a signal for them go back inside.

"Do you know why I told you this story?" He asked. They fell in step together, heading back to the office.

"I think I do." Amir said. "But why don't you tell me, just so I'm sure."

"I told you so you'd know I didn't start out knowing anything." Russell said. "I told you so you wouldn't worry so much."

"You know, earlier today I was pretty nervous." Amir said. He rubbed the back of his head. "I think I scared Nancy a bit. I was stressing over a toaster, of all things."

Russell laughed. He slapped Amir on the back. "You'll do just fine leading this company. Just remember you're not alone. And, of course, don't forget to check your blind spots."

Afterword: Working with Athena

I love working with professional trainers.

I think certain types of work generally attract certain types of people. The type of people attracted to coaching are usually great to be around: they're passionate about their specialty, they're always trying to give more to their clients, and they're generally really easy to make friends with. Also, they work really hard, which is something I admire—even though I try to do as little of it as possible.

That's why I was so pleased when Cindy Stradling asked me to write Blind Spots.

Over a period of four months, I worked on and off on this project with Cindy and the rest of the Athena Alliance. I met with them for coffee, I phoned them at all hours, and I drafted page after page of draft copies for them to review. The end result was Blind Spots, the book you just finished reading.

But actually, the work I did was next to nothing: Blind Spots was really written by eleven professionals from different backgrounds and specialties, united by their dedication to their craft, and to other people.

These are some pretty neat people. I learned a lot from each of them, and if I ever need help, I know they'll be my first stop for advice.

If you'd like to learn more about the Alliance, and I suggest you do, I suggest you check out the About the Authors section at the back of the book.

Amir Ahmed

Afterword: Working With Writers

Working with Amir has been a wonderful experience. When the alliance members and I first decided to write this book, we explored a variety of ways to do this. Once we decided that hiring a ghostwriter would be our best option, I was a little unsure how it would actually work. After all, we had ten different alliance members, three friends of the alliance and twelve different topics. I knew it would take someone that was not only a great writer, but also creative and flexible.

Our co-author and alliance member Claire Sookman introduced me to Amir. From our first conversation, I knew he was a fit for our project. Amir worked with our team with patience and creativity. He accepted changes and feedback with grace and it was clear he was dedicated to the success of this book.

On behalf of myself and the alliance members, thank you Amir for your professionalism and hard work. You were a delight to work with, and it was no small feat keeping our book "Blind Spots" on track. We wish you continued success!

Cindy Stradling CSP, CPC
Founder Athena Training and Consulting Inc.

About the Authors

SHERRI AUGER-GALLER

Sherri has made it her life's work to source and understand all of the options available to families with sick and dying relatives. In 2001, she left her burgeoning career and founded her own organization, determined to help others through one of the most difficult times of their lives. Since then, Sherri and her team have helped countless families provide the best possible care for their aging relatives. Sherri and  her team assists with all steps in the aging and illness process, including accessing government benefits and helping with the settling of estates.

DAVID BOYCE

As a corporate trainer, David provides performance solutions that advance organizational and individual performance. David understands the need for individuals and organizations to continually exceed past performance in employee, customer and stakeholder value. David's twenty years of experience leading growth and development initiatives within Canadian and global organizations forms the  foundation for his understanding of the unique performance requirements of each client.

SUSAN GREGORY

Susan Gregory is an independent corporate trainer and facilitator. She's travelled across Europe, the Middle East, and North America, teaching tools that develop communication, productivity, and creativity in the workplace. Susan believes that creating a fun and dynamic learning environment enhances a team's ability to learn, and inspires them to apply their lessons in the workplace. She is the former president of City of London Toastmasters in the UK.

DOROTHY LAZOVIK

Dorothy has worked with CEO's, directors and executives across fifteen different industries, helping them thrive in all areas of their lives. Dorothy excels at helping clients to know who they are, live with passion, play to their strengths and most importantly—own it! In 2008 and 2009, Dorothy was nominated for the RBC Canadian Woman Entrepreneur Award. She provides mentoring in developing effective Mastermind groups that support the career development of young female professionals.

JULIE RUBEN RODNEY

Julie Ruben Rodney is an expert in people development. She partners with clients to help them successfully execute their corporate strategy by maximizing the performance of their people. Julie is an experienced instructional designer, a dynamic facilitator and leading edge consultant in the areas of interpersonal communications, teambuilding, leadership development and creativity. Julie has a master's degree in adult education, specializing in workplace learning and change. She is a Certified Human Resources Professional (CHRP) and has the accreditation and experience to deliver a variety of assessment tools. Julie is passionate about engaging people to maximize their performance using a fun and positive approach.

CLAIRE SOOKMAN

Claire Sookman brings to the table over a decade's worth of corporate training experience. Specializing in virtual team building and communication strategies, Claire's unique, targeted approach has helped her clients increase productivity and efficiency of project teams. Her seminars have garnered numerous accolades, putting her services in high demand throughout North America. Claire's polished communication and training skills were honed though both practical and educational channels including a Master Trainer Certification through Langevin Learning Services. When not traveling for business or pleasure, Claire enjoys equestrian pursuits and other physical activities.

CINDY STRADLING

Author, facilitator, coach, keynote speaker, and founder of Athena Training and Consulting Inc.. Cindy Stradling has over twenty-five years of practical, hands-on business experience across various sectors. She is enthusiastic about strengthening her client's most powerful asset: their employees. Cindy has achieved her professsional sales designation (CSP) through the Canadian Professional Sales Association and she is a certified coach with Erickson College. She is a member of the International Coaching Federation and Canadian Professional Sales Association.

Cindy is passionate about the positive impact training and coaching has within organizations. She is a true connector and has created a powerful alliance of trainers, coaches and consultants providing clients with the "Perfect Fit" for their professional development needs.

CARROL SUZUKI

Carrol Suzuki is one of North America's premier business and workplace listening coaches and facilitators. She has developed seminars and coaching that appeals to professionals, leaders and teams in the fields of business, health care, law and the social services. She has worked in both the nonprofit and profit sectors as a hands-on and strategic manager, savvy organizational leader and trusted colleague. She brings a quiet but deep commitment to individual and team performance and success.

DEAN TURNER

Dean has an extensive background in First Aid, complimented by years of community service and consulting experience. Dean began his career as a First Aid instructor with the Department of National Defense, where he spent 12 years training soldiers for overseas duties. Dean is a Master Trainer for the Industrial Accident Prevention Association's (IAPA) Young Worker Awareness Program and is a member of their Executive Committee Board. He is a certified Instructor with the Royal Lifesaving Society and an Instructor Trainer for many levels of First Aid Training for the Canadian Red Cross.

GEOFF WEINSTEIN

Geoff Weinstein Defined
(jeff-wine-stine) n.
1. an easy-going guy who makes learning fun.
2. a passionate instructor.
3. a former corporate employee who slogged through difficult communications for 15 years.
4. husband, and father of three.

AMIR AHMED (Friend of the Alliance)

Amir doesn't like to talk about himself too much, but what the heck, here goes.

Amir is a wandering writer. He travels far and wide, completing writing projects, and proselytizing the em dash. He studied writing and communication in university, and the experience taught him to love clear, honest communication. He tries not to touch buzzwords without protective gear. Outside of work, Amir enjoys writing, running, and martial arts. His most heartfelt goals include writing bad fantasy novels, outracing his dad in a marathon, and one day throwing a proper punch.

AARON PEDERSON (Friend of the Alliance)

Aaron is a freelance writer and sub-contractor copywriter. After graduating from University with a focus on writing and philosophy, he did some internship work for Claire Sookman of Virtual Team Builders. Now he writes web-copy for sincere businesspeople and takes on other creative assignments and projects. In his spare time, Aaron enjoys reading, blogging, and playing beer league ice hockey. His biggest career goal is writing a novel that might be worthy of life outside a desk drawer.

STEPHEN SHEDLETZKY (Friend of the Alliance)

Stephen believes in a world in which the vast majority of people are fulfilled by the work they do. He leads inspirAction.ca, and collaborates with Simon Sinek's team at Start With Why—an organization that exists to inspire people to do the things that inspire them. Stephen engages leaders and organizations to discover and create their "Why"—their higher purpose that provides the clarity needed for fulfillment. He speaks, coaches, consults and creates content all with one purpose: to inspire. Stephen has received leadership and coaching training with the Richard Ivey School of Business and the Coaches Training Institute.

www.ingramcontent.com/pod-product-compliance
Lightning Source LLC
Chambersburg PA
CBHW030758180526
45163CB00003B/1072